Personal Tools for Success

U2Uni

Personal Tools for Success
4th Edition

Pearson Australia
707 Collins Street
Melbourne VIC 3008
www.pearson.com.au

www.pearson.com.au

Project Management Team Leader: Jill Gillies
Production Manager: Lisa D'Cruz
Custom Portfolio Manager: Lucie Bartonek
Portfolio Associate: Eleanor Yeoell
Production Controller: Dominic Harman

ISBN: 978 1 4886 2680 7

Table of contents

CHAPTER 2   Get it Write!
Structure your writing

About This Custom Book

This is a custom book of the original developed by Swinburne University. This customised version has been specifically adapted for Flinders University.

Dr Amanda Müller has been essential to the adaptation of this guide for Flinders University. She has meticulously checked the layout and the examples used and has made the necessary adjustments to make this book a perfect fit for the students of Flinders University.

Dr Amanda Müller is also a contributing author for this custom publication as her original material has been included in this compilation.

We hope you find this book very useful and informative.

This compilation also includes content from the following contributing authors:

Lester Faigley
Andy Gillet, Angela Hammond & Mary Martala
Ann Hogue
Barbara Kozier et al.
Lorraine Marshall
Amanda Müller
Alice Oshima & Ann Hogue

1 Be Adventurous!

Negotiate academic environments

Learning Outcomes

By the end of this chapter you will have strategies which enable you to:

> adapt successfully to change
> design, manage and monitor your learning
> apply your prior skills and knowledge to a new context
> identify your learning styles
> select and implement active learning strategies
> work collaboratively with others.

Studying at university makes very different demands on you compared to school or vocational colleges. As a student at university, you are required to take responsibility for your own learning. This transition may seem daunting when you have been used to a more teacher-guided approach.

Nevertheless, if you are an active learner you will find that the transition to university is less overwhelming. It is likely that you will find it to be a most rewarding, fulfilling and empowering experience. Active learning is an investment in your future, providing you with the skills and knowledge to be successful within the university environment and in the workplace.

Transition to university life

At university you will become aware that the environment and the expectations will be different from your previous educational experiences: Table 1.1 provides an overview of the contrasting features between a vocational college environment and a university environment.

What will university life be like?

Table 1.1 Vocational college/university overview

	Vocational college	University
Learning approach	› Vocational/practical focus and application	› Theoretical and analytical focus
Where and when students learn	› Mostly formal study in class/workshop	› Mostly independent study outside of contact hours
Time management	› Timetable arranged for you – you just turn up! › More contact hours per week	› Self-management of your timetable › The onus is on you to turn up! › Minimal contact hours per week
Class hours and size	› Fixed timetable and more class hours › Smaller class sizes › Study with same group of students throughout course › Attendance is monitored	› Timetable is flexible, with some lectures repeated › Large lecture groups › Student groups may vary with each topic › Self-management of attendance
Learning environment	› Teacher-facilitated learning › Ongoing feedback › Supported learning	› Support provided by academic staff when requested › Feedback less frequent › Self-directed adult learning

Table 1.1 Vocational college/university overview *continued*

	Vocational college	University
Amount of independent study	› Generally, 1-hour class = 30 minutes of independent study	› Generally, 1-hour lecture = at least 2 hours of independent study
Assessment expectations	› Practical application of knowledge and skills acquired › Acceptable responses clearly delineated by teacher › Flexibility with resubmission	› Analysis, evaluation and connections are made between current knowledge and new learning › Broader range of acceptable responses challenging ideas and theories › Less flexibility with resubmission – marking is more formalised

Accept that change brings challenges.

Overall, university expectations are different compared to vocational college or school. Consequently, you are required to take a much more *active* role in your learning in order to be successful. This enables you to develop skills and attributes which will greatly enhance your prospects for career, employment and future learning.

Graduate attributes include the ability to:

- be resourceful
- be organised
- work with others or alone
- communicate in a variety of ways and environments
- be analytical in your approach to problem solving
- evaluate information for future use
- employ a range of technologies
- research ethically and gather relevant information
- be creative and express ideas in a selection of formats.

Making the transition from vocational college or school to university may appear daunting yet exciting. You will discover that by choosing to adapt successfully to this change, you will become innovative, enterprising and resourceful. Developing a positive approach to your learning will facilitate the transformation. This course of action will include:

> creating and managing your own lecture and tutorial timetables
> planning and organising your independent study routine to meet deadlines
> being punctual to all lectures, tutorials and group sessions
> regularly checking communications such as your university email
> reading prescribed texts
> keeping up-to-date with your tutorial and lecture pre-reading requirements
> acting ethically and responsibly in preparing and submitting your assignments
> seeking help – not floundering or leaving your work until the last minute
> responding to constructive feedback
> reflecting on your learning progress
> treating all students and academic staff with respect.

Taking charge of your own learning takes planning, consideration, motivation, hard work and a determination to seek help when the journey becomes tough. An understanding of the learning environments at university will greatly assist you in developing this proactive attitude to your learning.

Negotiating the university learning environments

University culture

Every university environment has its own culture. Some have a very formal culture, whereas others are more relaxed. University cultures are centred around learning, with the focus on academic discussions and robust debate. Coupled with the academic culture are the social and multicultural aspects, which enrich the university experience.

You will meet and work collaboratively with others from socially, culturally and linguistically diverse backgrounds whose traditions and cultural outlooks may be very unfamiliar or different from your own. This aspect of university life widens the scope of your learning and provides you with the opportunity to understand and appreciate the value of diverse perspectives and outlooks. Enhancing your communication skills and your ability to work effectively with others greatly equips you to become an effective global citizen demonstrating respect and inclusiveness; this is particularly relevant in today's globally interconnected community.

Services available to students

At university there are many clubs and interest groups where you can meet others with similar interests. It is rewarding to build friendships and networks by engaging in formal or informal social activities in conjunction with the learning. Participating in university activities allows you to take a break from your formal learning and engage in social and/or cultural activities with others across disciplines, where you can relax, re-energise, make new friends and have fun. This is an important part of university life, as it can provide you with a support network which will enhance your wellbeing and further motivate and encourage you in your learning.

In addition, universities have a wide variety of support services and facilities, including:

> learning and academic skills support
> peer mentoring
> student counselling
> health services
> student housing information
> financial advice .
> bookshop
> IT support
> discount offers
> employment opportunities.

Each of these amenities provides an invaluable service to students. Investigate who and where they are at your university so that you can easily access them.

Flinders University provides on-campus health, counselling and disability services. They are located on level 3, Student Services Centre (next to the Sports Centre), North Ridge Precinct: http://www.flinders.edu.au/current-students/healthandcounselling/

Health service

The University provides a general practice medical service for students. It is open weekdays from 8.45 am–5.00 pm. You can ring (08) 8201 2118 for an appointment, book an appointment online (http://flinders.edu.au/current-students/healthandcounselling/health-service/health-service_home.cfm) or drop in and speak to the reception staff.

Counselling service

Counsellors are available to help manage the academic and personal welfare of all students enrolled at Flinders University. This may include assisting students who are struggling to manage their workloads and meet deadlines in a range of topics. The principal objective of counselling is to ensure that every student accepted for a course is given a reasonable and equitable opportunity to fulfil the academic and practical requirements of that course. The counselling service is free for students. The service is open on weekdays from 8.45am to 5.00pm Monday to Friday. If you want to make an appointment to see a counsellor, ring (08) 8201 2118 or email counselling@flinders.edu.au.

Students with disabilities

If you have a disability and require assistance or information, please contact a disability adviser in Health, Counselling and Disability Services. ('Disability' can be a medical condition, mental health condition, learning difficulty, or any disability that impacts on study.) The disability advisers provide a free, confidential service for enrolled students who have a disability; they are the first point of contact for information and assistance. The service is open Monday to Friday and you can ring (08) 8201 2118 or book an online appointment via the website. Their email address is disability@flinders.edu.au. Their website is http://flinders.edu.au/current-students/healthandcounselling/disability-services/disability-service_home.cfm.

The Flinders University Student Association (FUSA) is located at Level 1 of the student hub and helps students by providing advice, advocacy, grants, small scholarships and help with financial planning, employment and accommodation. FUSA also manages social and sports clubs. Go to www.fusa.edu.au.

If you need help with things like enrolment, exams, ID cards, etc., go to Flinders Connect under the library on the central campus or https://www.flinders.edu.au/flindersconnect.

Library

Knowledge of your university library and an appreciation for all it offers are essential to your success. Your library membership is accessed through your student identification card and may be expanded to include access to other university libraries through the CAVAL borrowing system. University libraries offer a vast array of support materials and services apart from their extensive collections of books, journals, databases, DVDs and multimedia. There are also many useful learning spaces available within the library which cater for individual or group study; explore these to find an area that you feel most comfortable in to supplement your study routine.

However, the most valuable resources within the library are the librarians, who have an extensive and specific knowledge of the university's various discipline areas. Generally, there will be a Liaison Librarian for each discipline, who will suggest the best resources for your assessments; ensure that you identify the Liaison Librarian for your area. Additionally, the library will provide workshops, including research skills training, the use of referencing systems and databases, and advice about plagiarism. Attending these workshops enables you to develop a sound understanding of these research and study skills while providing you with practical strategies to implement them.

Use the facilities and services provided by your university library; you will be surprised at what is available.

Flinders University Library

Four libraries are located on campus; each has student computers with access to the internet. You will need your student ID card to use many library facilities. Students enrolled on-campus will receive a card as part of the enrolment process. Students enrolled off-campus need to contact the Flexible Delivery Librarian to arrange a student ID card to be made and sent to their address.

The most accessible library for nursing and midwifery students is the Sturt Library. It can be accessed from level 3 at the southern end of the Sturt Precinct buildings. The Sturt Library holds library tours and training sessions about the use of library resources at the beginning of each year and at other times during the year. Please contact the Sturt Library for further information on 1300 354 633 (Select 3).

Sturt Library website: https://libraryflin.flinders.edu.au/about/branches/sturt-library

Library website: www.flinders.edu.au/library

Topic details

Successfully negotiating every aspect of the university learning environment will require you to have a comprehensive understanding of each topic you are enrolled in. Important information about your subjects will be found in the individual topic details. You will need to *refer to your topic details continually* throughout the semester.

> The topic details will be your study 'companion', which informs and guides your learning.

The topic details contains a **plethora** of information about the subject to which you will need to refer frequently. It is therefore strongly recommended that you keep your topic details handy for quick reference. It will not only provide you with a clear overview of your topic, but will incorporate information pertaining to:

> lecturer and tutor contact details
> methods of communication and how to get help
> lecture and tutorial structure
> required and recommended texts
> minimum requirements to pass the topic

> submission of assignments
> assessment tasks
> guidelines around plagiarism, team work and appeals procedure
> sundry items relating to the specific topic.

Referring to your topic details regularly will ensure that you comply with all the requirements to pass the topic.

Flinders nursing degrees website

The Flinders nursing degrees website (http://www.flinders.edu.au/nursing/) contains up-to-date information about courses, clinical placements, Sturt and Riverland facilities, academic integrity, research projects, staff in the College and much more. Resources for students are available at the following website: http://www.flinders.edu.au/nursing/studentsandcourses/resources-for-students/resources-for-students.cfm#.

FLO topic websites

Topic websites and links to support materials are accessed through FLO. To access your site for a particular topic, log in to FLO at: https://flo.flinders.edu.au/.

The student companion provides information about courses, services, computer access, FLO, clinical placements, assignments, exams, policies, student appeals, and more. Link to it from https://flo.flinders.edu.au/enrol/index.php?id=9074.

A guide to clinical placement provides information about clinical placement, performance requirements, placement options, placement notification, preparing for placement, attendance, assessment, and support. Link to it from http://www.flinders.edu.au/nursing/professional-experience-placements/

Professional Language Development is a topic mainly aimed at international students and provides information about how to develop your Nursing English, links to self-test quizzes, computer games, medical terminology help, writing help, and much more. Link to it from https://flo.flinders.edu.au/course/view.php?id=4234.

Lectures

Lectures are held in large spaces often known as lecture theatres, which can accommodate hundreds of students. It is possible that you may not know some

of the students sitting around you. In the lecture theatre your personal space is limited; there is little room for extra books or bags and only a small area provided for taking notes. (This might be a narrow bench or fold-up table.) The theatre is usually tiered and the seats are close together, making moving around once the lecture starts unlikely!

Unlike at vocational college or school, your attendance at lectures is not recorded. However, as an active learner, you will gain a greater understanding from attending a lecture, discussing the topic with others and asking questions. Lectures may be recorded, but recordings are best used as a revision tool. Students who make full use of the face-to-face contact at lectures generally achieve their learning goals.

Choose where you sit wisely!

Consider the following constructive strategies for lecture behaviour:
> Arrive early – this not only minimises your anxiety about the lecture beginning before you are seated, but it also shows respect to the lecturer and your fellow students!
> Sit near the front to greatly improve your chances of seeing and hearing. (Even though technology significantly enables this process, it is still advisable to sit near the front.)
> Scan your lecture handout (if provided) before the lecture to gain an overview.
> Use the lecture handout (if provided) to guide your note taking.
> Minimise your movement once the lecture has begun, as interruptions are disruptive and distract everyone.
> Turn your phone and devices to silent mode.

Mug to go: Bring your own water bottle and coffee cup. Plastic, styrofoam and wax-coated cups don't biodegrade and create landfill.

The purpose of lectures and the role of lecturers

In general, the purpose of a lecture is to provide you with an overview of the topic content as well as an analysis of the theory related to that topic. In a lecture, the lecturer will:

> outline the order in which the topic will be covered
> emphasise important points to focus on and for you to research further
> provide you with other references and sources of information to investigate
> stimulate your own thinking around the topic
> encourage you to critically analyse the topic in more detail
> provide you with an insight into new, unpublished research theories
> suggest practical ways to consider the topic
> provide you with a summary of the content covered throughout the semester before exams.

Having said this, individual lecturers will adapt the lecture delivery style to suit the desired purpose. Lecturers will, however, provide you with clues as to the content, purpose and the structure of a particular lecture. It will be up to you, as an active learner, to look for these clues.

Remember that each lecturer will have their own delivery style: it may take you time to become familiar with it. Traditionally, the lecture-style format focuses on the lecturer as the deliverer of knowledge, with the lecturer standing before the class and presenting information for the students to absorb. This usually means that there is very little interaction or exchange between the lecturer and students.

Many innovative lecturers are now more aware of the need not only to instruct their students, but also to engage them with the same passion they hold for their subject. Their ability to do this, of course, depends on their personality. So, as an active learner, you must be prepared for all methods and styles of learning!

Furthermore, it is important to be aware of the role lecturers have at university: often, lecturing makes up only a very small part of their academic role. Frequently, lecturers are involved in time-consuming research projects, publishing articles for academic journals, supervising postgraduate students with their research and sitting on academic boards and committees.

It is useful to appreciate that lecturers' roles are many and varied. They will not have the time to 'chase' students for assignments! More often than not, lecturers are quite happy to share their knowledge and expertise with students who show an interest, but it is up to you to make the appointment!

Structure of lectures

Lectures, like any aspect of academic writing or presentation, will generally follow a clear format incorporating an introduction, body and conclusion. Some lecturers also include a summary of the issues raised, towards the end of the lecture. It is essential that you attend the lecture in its entirety. Arriving late will mean that you miss the most important part of the lecture: the introduction, which not only provides you with an overview of the content and the perspective being taken, but also sets the **context** for the rest of the lecture.

Following the introduction, the lecturer will develop the main points and present an analysis of the theory related to that subject, using evidence, research data and examples to validate the

perspective taken. It is important for you to listen carefully in order to understand and take relevant notes. Some lecturers will indicate significant points for you to remember: use these clues to guide your note taking (see Table 1.2).

Listen for clues given by the lecturer as a guide to your note taking.

In concluding the lecture, the lecturer will reinforce the purpose of the lecture, sum up the main points and deliver a final perspective on the theory. There may be an opportunity for questions.

Table 1.2 Active learning strategies for lectures

Prior to the lecture
1. Complete any prescribed reading relating to the lecture topic.
2. Discuss it with other students to reinforce your basic understanding of the topic and become familiar with the main ideas.
3. Familiarise yourself with the subject-specific terminologies and vocabulary to increase your ability to understand and spell new words.
4. Decide how you wish to record your notes during the lecture.
5. Record the date, title of the lecture and the full name of the lecturer.
6. Find out how the lecture notes/presentation will be made available to you.

During the lecture
7. Use your active listening skills to help you decide what information to record.
8. Write down the main points as emphasised by the lecturer.
9. Use diagrams, pictures or tables to help you recall the information.
10. Record any questions or points to clarify.
11. Listen actively and involve yourself in understanding what is being said.

After the lecture
12. Write down as much of what you remember about the content while it is still fresh in your mind.
13. Within 24 hours, read over your notes to ensure that they make sense.
14. Rewrite or type your notes, if this makes rereading them easier.
15. Write down or highlight any information that needs further clarification.
16. Identify any gaps you have in your notes.
17. Correct any spelling mistakes, including names of people or resource details.
18. Make links in your notes between what you already know and the new information.
19. Regularly review your lecture notes so that the information is embedded in your long-term memory.
20. Review the lecture via podcast or vodcast if available.

Tutorials

At university you will be required to attend tutorials, which are frequently referred to as 'tutes'. These are usually 2 hours in length and occur on a regular, weekly, or bi-weekly basis. The tutorials take place in classrooms around the campus; this means that you may not always have your tutorial in a building relating to your course.

There can be up to 30 students in a tutorial; but usually the number is around 25. The tutorial will be led by a tutor, who is a member of the academic faculty and may be a permanent or casual staff member.

Although it is difficult to be specific, there are differences between a lecture and a tutorial. A lecture gives you an overview of the subject content and theory related to that subject, whereas a tutorial gives you the opportunity to discuss the content of the lecture within a more relaxed and informal setting. To gain the most out of your tutorial, it is highly recommended that you:

> arrive on time
> choose where you sit wisely
> bring your lecture notes, handouts, annotated reading material and questions.
> turn your phone and devices to silent mode.

Drive less: car pool, use public transport, walk or ride a bike. All of these alternatives to driving your own car are not only good for the environment; they are great for your health.

The purpose of tutorials and the role of tutors

The nature of tutorials will vary from tutor to tutor and topic to topic; but overall, tutorials will give you the chance to:

> explore and clarify the topic
> ask questions
> practise your active listening skills

> interact with other students
> develop your critical understanding of the topic content
> formulate and express opinions
> debate the issues
> understand how the theory relates to the topic
> review your progress
> develop study groups.

The role of the tutorial leader is to promote discussion; facilitate debate, clarify information, encourage students to explore ideas and mentor them in their academic work.

Always be respectful when working with others.

Table 1.3 Active learning strategies for tutorials

Prior to the tutorial
1. Attend the relevant lecture.
2. Review your lecture notes.
3. Complete the required pre-reading and preparatory activities.
4. Take notes.
5. Jot down ideas and any questions.

During the tutorial
6. Use active listening skills and take notes.
7. Participate and contribute by sharing your views and asking questions.
8. Stay focused.
9. Use appropriate language.
10. Demonstrate respect and be inclusive.
11. Be open to change.
12. Explore alternatives.
13. Learn from each other.
14. Appreciate the value of others.
15. Work collaboratively.
16. Be prepared to lead a discussion or activity.

After the tutorial
17. Review your notes.
18. Follow up on any issues raised.
19. Identify where you need to do further research.
20. Form a study group.
21. Attend follow-up workshops when provided.
22. Make an appointment with your tutor if required.
23. Complete the set tutorial tasks in readiness for your next tutorial.

FLO (Flinders Learning Online)

Each university will have a website which holds information about the university online. As a student you will have access to parts of the university website that are not available to the public. These are known as student learning management systems and will be unique to every university.

Flinders University has Flinders Learning Online, or FLO. FLO holds resources that are relevant to every stage of your learning journey; everything from initial enrolment and topic selection to learning how to research and access potential graduate employment opportunities. The university will use the learning management system to keep you informed and to provide you with essential documentation. FLO holds a vast range of electronic resources, including podcasts, digital recordings of lectures, online tutorials and student guides.

FLO is an essential source of information for you as a student. It is here that you will access:

> lecture handouts and
>   PowerPoint presentations
> topic coodinator, lecturer
>   and tutor announcements
> topic outlines
> required reading lists
> assessment tasks
> assessment guidelines
> marking guides/rubrics
> self-directed study materials
> academic study support
> professional language
>   development
> library services.

FLO is designed to be interactive and incorporate a range of learning tools to assist your learning. These might include discussion forums, reflective journals, blogs, podcasts, lecture recordings and links to other websites. FLO is used for a number of purposes, where you will:

> submit assignments
> contribute to online discussions
> maintain a reflective journal
> watch lectures
> communicate with your topic coordinator, lecturer, tutor or peers
> access prescribed readings and online activities.

You may have the opportunity to enrol in an online topic. This will require careful consideration in deciding whether this method of learning suits you. The benefits of online study include flexibility around when and how you engage in the topic content. However, be aware that undertaking an online topic will bring a different set of challenges and incorporate different expectations. You will need to investigate what the topic entails and determine whether you have the technology, the skills and the time to engage in the topic in this format. It will also require an autonomous, disciplined approach to your learning. Remember that whilst it may seem appealing to enrol in an online topic and not attend classes, this learning environment still requires the same time commitment as all other topics. Plan your personal study timetable to coordinate a regular time to go online and be an active participant.

Online topics will generally include mandatory lecture vodcasts, prescribed readings, discussion forums and possibly reflective journal entries. They may also incorporate additional readings, links to further sources of information, quizzes, assignments and a portal for submitting assessment tasks. FLO records your participation each time you log on, and is used by the tutor and topic coordinator to confirm your involvement in the topic. Your entries can be monitored by the tutor, who will mentor students in this learning environment.

Will online learning and study suit me? How will I successfully negotiate this environment?

Student FANs

When you first enrol at Flinders University you are automatically issued with a Flinders Authentication Name (FAN) and a default password. Your FAN and its associated password give you access to many University electronic services, including FLO, email, your personal library account and the student information system. Information about activating your FAN can be found here: https://askflinders .microsoftcrmportals.com/article/KA-05308/en-us

Topic websites are accessed through FLO. To access your site for a particular topic, log in to FLO at: https://flo.flinders.edu.au/.

Etiquette in an online environment: 'Netiquette'

Guidelines are set by the university for online communications, such as within emails and on FLO, and will incorporate issues such as the following:

> Use appropriate language.
> Maintain focus on the topic.
> Remain unemotional and non-judgemental of others.
> Always be respectful and inclusive when working with others.
> Keep an open mind.
> Appreciate and learn from your online peers.
> Participate fully in discussions.
> Be prepared to engage in robust debate.
> Extend your academic vocabulary.
> Use an appropriate tone to express your views; this may be more difficult in a written format.
> Be guided by your tutor as you learn.

You can access the College's 'social media guidelines and netiquette' through the Student Companion link on your FLO topic site, or go to it directly: http://flinders.edu.au/nursing/student-resources/social-media-guidelines-and-netiquette.cfm

Use appropriate language that reflects good manners.

Learning online can be challenging and may seem artificial when you compare it to attending a tutorial. In a tutorial you explore a topic, listen and contribute whilst physically being with others. This allows you to observe the non-verbal body language of your peers to support your understanding of the issue. This non-verbal communication is not evident in an online forum and requires different strategies to successfully negotiate.

Online environments can include both synchronous (live chat or instant messaging, virtual classrooms) and asynchronous (blogs, discussion forums and wikis) media. Asynchronous communications are beneficial as they are accessible at whatever time of day suits. The use of asynchronous media provides the flexibility for you to access readings and blogs when it is convenient for you in preparation for tutorials, lectures and online discussions. You need to be aware, however, that you may need to wait for feedback on your comments in an online environment. Conversely, synchronous media tools provide an instant response and, in the university online environment, may also include the use of specialist software and webcams, or video-conferencing such as Skype.

You can cut your energy use by 70 per cent using an energy-saving setting, switching the computer off when you are not using it and not setting up a screensaver.

Active strategies for online learning
- Navigate and explore your online topic resources, links, discussions and assessments to give yourself an overview of the environment.
- Investigate the prescribed readings to complement your learning:
    o Complete the additional tasks that are posted.
    o Access weblinks.
    o Listen to podcasts.
    o Review lectures.
    o View vodcasts.
- Participate often: sign in regularly and make a point of contributing to discussion forums.
- Ask questions of your tutor and peers to clarify information; this will encourage others to speak up and develops trust.
- Ask your tutor for help as soon as you need it.
- Request assistance from the IT Help Desk if the technology is unreliable or you cannot access a particular file.
- Take advantage of opportunities to interact synchronously via chat, webinars, Skype or virtual classrooms.

Be an active online learner: join in the discussions, become involved and make connections with others.

Having made a choice to learn at university, you will engage in the steps of a Conscious Learning Cycle. Your focus will be on the academic requirements of your course of study, which will guide how you take in and use the information. Figure 1.1 illustrates how this process unfolds through receiving, considering, assessing and then acting on information.

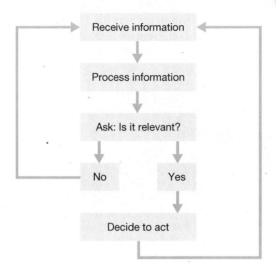

Figure 1.1 Conscious Learning Cycle

Learning styles

It is a problem when students think that the only way they learn is 'by doing'. In fact, you learn for different reasons and in a variety of ways.

At university you will work with others who prefer to learn in different ways to you. Being aware of this is the first step towards not only understanding your *own* learning and applying effective learning strategies, but also realising that others have different preferences which you will need to respect.

In the academic environment, considerable research has been conducted which has explored different ways of learning. Honey and Mumford (1982), Gardner

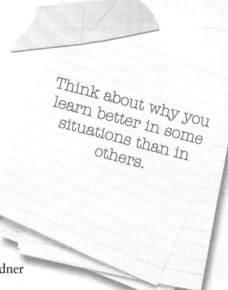

Think about why you learn better in some situations than in others.

(1993), Kolb (1984), Lave and Wenger (1998), to name just a few, have developed theories which reveal how information is gathered, organised and used in different ways. These learning theories are models of learning. Having an overview of the models gives you insight and helps you to clarify your own preferred style of learning. Identifying the many ways in which you learn best will enable you to manage your learning journey and become an empowered active learner.

You will find that exploring your own learning styles can be exciting and liberating. You will gain new insight into why and how you learn best, and this information will help you to succeed as a life-long learner in every situation.

Consider the information in Table 1.4. Do you recognise your learning preferences and particular skills? Highlight the statements that you believe best describe you.

Table 1.4 Learning preferences

I enjoy the creative process, rather than the implementation	I am a big picture person
I am open-minded	I look for new opportunities
I focus on the big picture	I like to try out new ideas
I am hands-on	I am down-to-earth
I am spontaneous	I like to practise what I learn
I enjoy challenges	I am goal-focused
I look at things from different angles	I focus on tasks
I am people-oriented	I like to develop plans for action
I can motivate others	I am logical
I enjoy learning by discovery	I am a decision-maker
I am resourceful	I am a problem-solver
I am self-reliant	I find practical solutions
	I look for better ways of doing things

I am thoughtful	I like structure
I stand back and observe before I act	I work through things in logical steps
I consider things carefully before moving on	I need to see the finer details
I draw conclusions after a lot of thought	I make connections between what I know and new information
I think before speaking up	I am objective
I consider all angles	I like to reason
I plan well to meet deadlines	I can develop ideas and theories to make connections
I gather information	I like to ask probing questions
I research and analyse before creating a response	I like to design projects (from theory to application)
I like to reflect on my learning	I can understand abstract concepts
I can focus on the detail while still seeing the big picture	I have a thirst for knowledge

It is possible to identify with characteristics from a variety of learning styles. Remember that it is important to develop strategies across all styles so that you will become more effective and successful in your learning.

Discover creative ways to enhance your learning experience.

Whilst the way you are taught can influence your learning, it is more important to identify how *you* respond as an active learner.

At university you will be exposed to many different learning situations and will need to implement a range of strategies

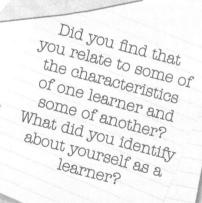

Did you find that you relate to some of the characteristics of one learner and some of another? What did you identify about yourself as a learner?

to make the information relevant to your learning. For example, if you enjoy the creative process and big picture ideas, you may find it challenging to concentrate on detail, whereas sequential learners prefer to start from the beginning and understand the details before proceeding.

> **If you are a big picture learner:** try brainstorming to record your ideas; working in teams; highlighting your notes; using colour; and adding visual images.
> **If you are a learner who prefers to learn step-by-step:** work with others to brainstorm ideas; paraphrase information; and develop graphics or diagrams to create an overview.

Selecting an appropriate strategy will give you the tools to meet the challenge.

Now think about your previous learning experiences.
· What helped you to be successful?
· Why? How did you overcome a difficult experience?
· Who inspired you?
· What motivated you to learn?

Be successful: focus on what *you* can do.

Be open to new ways of doing things.

By selecting a range of learning strategies, you actively engage in the Conscious Learning Cycle: effectively, you choose to maximise the opportunities available to you. This equips you to successfully self-direct and manage your own learning.

Here is a collation of active learning strategies across all learning styles. Highlight the ones which appeal to you and select others to try.

Take notes

Ask questions

Reflect on your learning

Use colours and highlighters to mark your text and own notes

Be an active listener

Be an active team member

Encourage and motivate others

Explore new ideas

Use a range of multimedia learning tools

Plan and organise your information

Be flexible

Be creative

Brainstorm your ideas

Be involved in discussions and debates

Share ideas

Have fun with your learning

Keep a diary

Connect what you know with new ideas

Keep a 'to do' list

Take one step at a time

Break large projects into smaller parts

Set realistic goals

Think things over

Review notes

Active learning

Active learners are self-reliant individuals who successfully manage their own learning. They are:

> enthusiastic
> involved
> empowered
> capable
> team players
> creative.

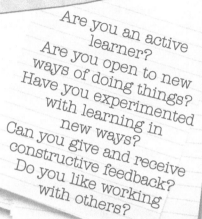

Are you an active learner?
Are you open to new ways of doing things?
Have you experimented with learning in new ways?
Can you give and receive constructive feedback?
Do you like working with others?

Table 1.5 lists a range of skills which accurately describe active learners. Developing and refining these skills will enhance your learning.

Are you still trying to decide if you are an active learner?

Remember: you have a choice. If you feel uncertain about your learning abilities and believe it is too hard, then it will be! If you choose to be challenged by the learning opportunity and take a proactive view, you will become more capable and confident in your ability to learn and will search for strategies to facilitate a positive learning journey.

'You have to expect things of yourself before you can do them.'
—*Michael Jordan*

However, if you need further convincing . . . being actively involved in your learning will:

> increase your concentration and motivation
> improve your listening and ability to take in new information
> heighten your self-esteem and belief in your capabilities
> positively affect your overall learning and enjoyment.

Nevertheless, it is important to realise that simply identifying with the title 'active learner' does not mean you *are* one. You need to have a real understanding of what it means. You will need to develop and master skills you already have and acquire new ones. This will ensure that you have the capacity to manage and direct your own learning using a variety of strategies.

In addition to using a range of learning strategies, active learners successfully employ a very 'hands-on' technique. This is called an Active Learning Approach, which involves practical, interrelated actions: to observe, explore, share and reflect

Table 1.5 Active learning skills

Active learners:
Are capable and confident in their ability to learn
Set goals
Break goals down into steps that are achievable and measurable
Design and negotiate their learning journey
Create, explore and test opportunities
Put contingency plans in place
Manage time
Demonstrate an active, healthy work, life, study balance

Gather Information
Ask questions
Analyse and evaluate information
Make informed decisions
Research and read widely
Apply what they already know
Make connections between what they know and new information
Use the resources available to them
Explore further
Are open to challenging their own and other perspectives

Are involved in their learning
Know how they like to learn
Adapt and use learning strategies to maximise their success
Take ownership of their learning journey
Are receptive to change
Look for ways to make their learning relevant

Recognise the benefits of collaboration
Interact with others
Empower others
Value others

(see Figure 1.2). Each of these actions interacts with the other and every part is essential. By implementing this approach to active learning, you will more confidently process, organise, apply and review new information. If you choose to use this learning approach, you will quickly discover that you develop an appreciation for the value of your learning, and an awareness of the knowledge and skills you are acquiring along the way. This is a rewarding, motivating and exciting experience, and one that can reveal new possibilities. Who knows where this will lead you?

Use the Active Learning Approach and broaden your horizons.

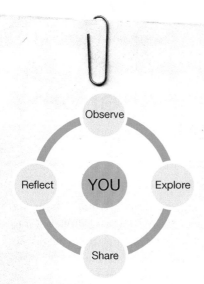

Figure 1.2 Active Learning Approach
Source: Adapted from Kolb's model of experiential learning (1984).

Even as an active learner you will face hurdles in your learning, or you may not reach your own or others' expectations. The challenge for you, as an active learner, is to face your obstacles and find strategies to manage them. Making mistakes is an important part of the learning process. Recognising that you *can* do it, but you don't know *how*, is what you explore.

Think about the new skills you will need to develop at university: critical thinking, reading, research and writing skills. How will you use the Active Learning Approach to establish an understanding and application of these skills?

Focus on what you *can* do, not on what you can't.

'Success consists of going from failure to failure without losing your enthusiasm.' —*Winston Churchill*

Every question you ask deepens your learning.

Transferring learning strengths into university study

Introduction

Usually when considering the transfer of knowledge and skills, we think about the process of transfer from an educational to a non-educational context. However, it is also possible to transfer skills and knowledge from a non-academic to an academic setting. You are constantly involved in the learning process, in learning new information or skills, but you probably rarely consider your prior learning or how you use your new learning. This exercise encourages you to transfer your learning to new situations by asking you to consider your learning strengths so that you can adapt and apply those that are appropriate to your study.

Many of the exercises in this book require that you consider if any of your previous learning experiences are relevant to the academic skills being developed. The following exercise asks you to reflect on your prior learning in formal situations, such as secondary school, and apply your knowledge of this learning to what is expected in university study. If possible complete this exercise with another student, friend or family member.

Learning activities

Previous learning experiences

Reflect on your previous learning experiences – perhaps at home, in a job, for a hobby or at school. Select a project in which you were involved and interested, where you learnt a lot and that was enjoyable and successful. In your learning log, briefly describe the project, what you learned and the skills involved.

Examples of informal learning projects include choosing a new car, negotiating a contract, learning to play tennis, fixing your car, raising a child, learning to scuba dive and so on.

A further example of an informal learning project might be learning to care for an aged relative. This could have involved you actually deciding what you needed to learn about caring for the aged, setting goals that you hoped to achieve for your relative, seeking information on health and other associated issues, and learning how to listen sympathetically.

Conditions that enhance your learning

Think of a past project and describe the conditions that helped you to learn. Try to be as specific as you can.

Consider and then describe how you can transfer your knowledge of how you learn into your study.

Your learning strengths

Draw up two columns. In the first column, list those learning skills that you consider to be your strengths. Don't restrict yourself here. Your strengths might be reading, planning parties, organising other people, working for extended times on topics of interest, using your hands, visualising, rote learning, parenting, following recipes, writing letters to the editor and so on.

In the second column, describe the origin of this skill and where it has been fostered.

Using an asterisk, identify those skills that you think might be useful in your university study. Which skills do you need to adapt, change or refine to fulfil the expectations of study at university?

If you are beginning tertiary study, you may find this question challenging. Remember that the formal learning environment of a tertiary institution may require that you modify present skills or develop new abilities.

Gaps in your learning experiences

Reflect on your life and think about any gaps in your life experiences that may have influenced your repertoire of skills. For example, perhaps you are an expert plumber and handy with your hands, but have little experience with book learning. Perhaps you were raised in a household with few books. Perhaps you spent a lot of time alone and are uncomfortable talking in groups. Perhaps you grew up in a family where listening to others was not the norm.

Discuss with a study partner(s) what you will do to overcome these gaps. For example, perhaps you can attend special classes, seek out appropriate material or work through the appropriate chapters in this book.

Active learning strategies

Manage your time

Throughout life you will need to manage a number of roles all at the same time: you may be a student, an employee, a family member, a friend and a team player. Managing these roles successfully involves planning and being well organised. It is essential that you prioritise your time to do the things that are important, including taking time to relax and sleep. Achieving a balance between the many aspects of your life, especially now that you are studying, is an important consideration for you as a successful, active learner.

Having made the decision to study, you need to prioritise and plan, allocating time to both your academic and personal life. There are only a finite number of hours in each day: if you do not have a plan in place you may waste time, miss deadlines or not complete important tasks. Planning and prioritising your time enables you to use your time effectively and efficiently.

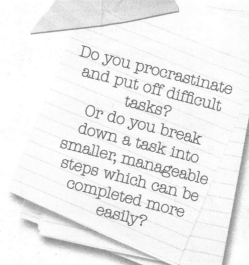

Do you procrastinate and put off difficult tasks? Or do you break down a task into smaller, manageable steps which can be completed more easily?

Consider this time management guide. Reflecting upon it will indicate how you currently use your time, and will highlight how you might use your time more efficiently in the future.

How do you spend your time during a typical 24-hour day? (Average your hours over an entire week: for example, you may work 11 hours per week – divide this by 7 to arrive at a daily average.)

1. Fill in the yellow column and total the number of hours.

Tasks	How much time per day do you allocate to this task?	Review
Sleeping		
Preparing food, eating meals and cleaning up		
Personal care and grooming (getting dressed, shower, toilet)		
Attending lectures/tutorials/classes		
Studying (independent study)		
Socialising		
Spending time with your family		
Relaxing		
Exercising		
Travelling		
Working		
Other		
Total		

2. Now look at your hours closely and consider the following:
   Have you run out of hours per day to do everything you need and want to do?
   Do you spend enough time sleeping?
   Have you allocated time to exercise?
   Have you included adequate time to study?
   Which areas have you allocated the most/least time to?

3. As you complete the review column (purple), think about these questions and aim for a realistic and achievable allocation of your time:

What *must* you do in a day (sleep, eat . . .)?

Are there activities you can cut back on? Can you identify areas where you may need to increase/decrease the time you spend on an activity?

Have you allowed for some exercise, sport or relaxation each day for your health and wellbeing?

4. Finally, reflect!

To which areas did you allocate more time? What influenced your decisions?

Considering your priorities and deciding how much time to allocate to your daily activities is an essential part of being an active learner. As you have chosen to study at university, you have made a commitment to learn and will want to do your best. Therefore, managing your time and prioritising your tasks are an important part of your new routine.

Reflect on how much time you will need to assign to study per day/per week.

Find an excuse to exercise! Remember that exercise is good for your body and your mind, and eating a healthy diet will help you to be an active learner! Without exercise and good nutrition, your body becomes tired and stressed and you study less effectively.

It is essential that you create enough time for the things that are important to your health, both physical and emotional, and to your work and study. Daily, weekly, monthly and/or semester planners are invaluable tools for developing a realistic strategy for managing your time.

As part of your Active Learning Approach, use a semester or monthly planner to mark in the important dates for assignment deadlines, exam schedules and other study submissions.

> Think about how much time you will need to allocate to each task in order to meet the deadlines.
> Consider the amount of time you will need for exam revision.
> Plan for unexpected events that may impact on your ability to complete a task.
> Allow yourself time to get fully involved, to enjoy the learning and to create pieces of work that demonstrate your skill and creativity!

Be organised and plan your work in advance.

Developing a weekly plan that includes study, lecture and tutorial time, along with the other commitments which are an integral part of your life, will help you to prioritise your tasks for each day. First consider tasks that must be done which are not negotiable; those that are less urgent may be shifted to another day. Some tasks will require more time than others. Smaller tasks can be achieved if you use your time creatively and more flexibly. For example, send an email from your phone while you are on the train or read through your notes whilst waiting for an appointment!

Keep your focus on the big picture: use a wall planner.
Maintain your focus on the details: keep a diary (hard copy or electronic).

Develop a study routine

As a result of using your daily and weekly planner, you can allocate regular study periods to your routine, including time for reading, exploring ideas, writing and participating in study groups. In developing a routine, you are making a commitment to your learning and allowing yourself the opportunity to be actively involved in your own learning journey. Be aware that leaving things until the last minute may cause you stress, sap your energy and compromise your joy of learning.

Semester 1

Year at a glance

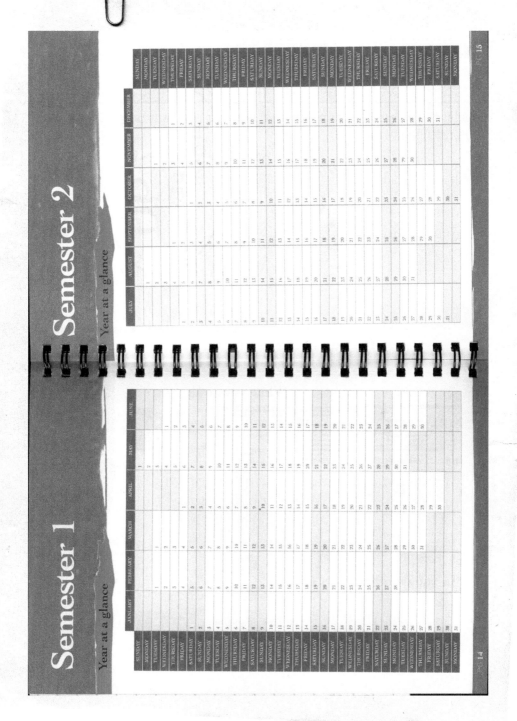

Semester 2

Year at a glance

Be creative with your study routine! Consider where you are most productive and engaged in your learning and make an effort to replicate those conditions wherever possible in your study routine.

activity 1.8

Look at the words below and circle those that best suit how and where you prefer to study.

Online

With a study buddy   **Alone**

Night owl   With minimal noise

With snacks

In the computer lab

Inside

Drinking coffee   **At your desk**

In the library

As you jog   **While you walk**

In short bursts

Music playing   Under a tree

With my study group

With others   Outside

In the cafeteria

Listening to your iPod

Over longer time   With a view

Early bird

> Think about the environment where you know you will be most productive. When you study you want to see results. Do you prefer to write notes, or to draw diagrams and pictures to represent ideas? Do you like to brainstorm so that you can explore ideas?

> What time of day works best for you? If you find you work best first thing in the morning, consider scheduling your independent study time then. However, if you find it easier to think at night, then schedule your work commitments for during the day and leave the evenings for study.

> Do you procrastinate when you start your study? If you sit at the computer to study but find that you get distracted by checking your emails or looking at social networking sites, consider whether this is the best use of your study time.

The key to a good study routine is to consider: Where, when, what and how do I study best?

Open a window and let in the fresh air rather than turn on the air conditioner.
Sit in the sun or put on another jumper before turning on the heater.
Fresh air and sunlight are nature's air conditioning and light.

Reward yourself and acknowledge your achievements.

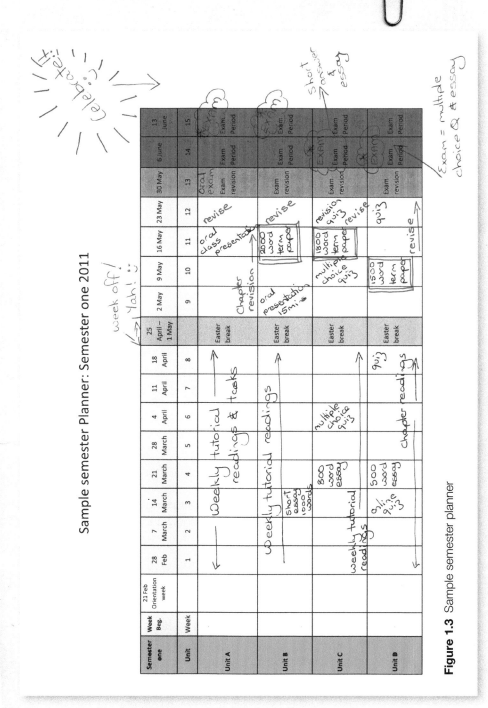

Figure 1.3 Sample semester planner

Ask yourself these questions:

What do I want to achieve?

Explore these ideas to identify specific goals. The more explicit your goal is, the more likely you are to develop a strategy to achieve it.

Why do I want to achieve it?

These insights will be a source of motivation to plan to meet your goal.

How can I achieve my goal?

Think creatively about how you can achieve it. Identify the smaller chunks to break it down into steps.

How will I know when I have achieved my goal?

Describe what will happen to demonstrate you have achieved your goal.

All about balance

University students frequently work whilst studying, in order to pay their daily costs of food, transport, housing, mobile phone, internet connection and social interactions. When you commit to studying at university, you will need to prioritise your time to ensure that you can successfully balance your study whilst juggling other commitments, such as work and social life. Occasionally you may need to adjust your paid work hours, particularly if you have assignments due or exams are looming. Nevertheless, achieving a work/study balance and managing your budget will help you to establish a plan to meet your financial commitments.

A study planner is an invaluable tool for managing all your commitments. In this, you can highlight when your study commitments will be the most demanding and identify the times when you may need to reduce your paid work hours. You will need to use your time wisely if you wish to achieve your goal and obtain a qualification: this will require you to allocate sufficient hours to study. Reducing your work hours, juggling bills and arranging expenses to manage any reduction in income may be challenging, but advanced planning and adhering to a budget, will minimise the possible stress. However, be aware that at university you do not have to cope alone.

Universities provide a number of specific services which offer support to students to assist them in managing their study, work and life balance. These support services may include: student counselling; financial advice and assistance with budgeting; housing and rental assistance; health and wellbeing information; disability support; as well as career and employment guidance. Student services will also provide advice regarding government financial provisions for students, and direct you to other relevant services which might save you money or provide extra income. Above all, focus on what you want to achieve and seek the advice or support you may require to maintain a healthy balance.

Manage stress

Throughout life you will face challenges on a daily basis which may cause you some stress. University study will bring its own set of challenges which may make you feel anxious: unfamiliar study environment; new people; different expectations; juggling work, study and home commitments.

There are a variety of physical reactions to stress, some of which include: clammy hands, dry mouth, feeling tired, headaches, lacking energy, not sleeping well, feeling sick or being emotional. If you can identify when your body is signalling stress, you may be able to gain some insight into the cause of that stress. This opens up the opportunity to develop strategies to minimise its impact. Stress can be a very subjective reaction: what stresses you may not stress someone else.

How do I manage stress?

Acknowledge that you feel stressed in some situations. This is the first step to managing your stress; nevertheless, it is also important to acknowledge that stress is not always negative. It is a natural human response. Listen to your body, seek help early with excessive stress, and above all be kind to yourself.

- Ensure you are eating well, getting plenty of sleep and exercising.
- Discuss your thoughts and feelings with others: friends, peers, family, academic staff, medical doctor or a student counsellor can open your eyes to a different perspective and encourage you.
- Plan and organise your time and study routines from the outset. Use your diary or weekly/semester planner and set goals to keep you focused and motivated.
- Choose a special study place that best suits the way you prefer to learn. This is a place where you feel comfortable, productive and inspired.
- Be an active learner and focus on positive outcomes.
- Review your goals and adjust your smaller goals to identify more manageable and achievable steps.
- Use relaxation techniques including yoga, breathing exercises or listening to calming music.
- Have fun with your study. Look for a variety of creative ways to bring fun into your learning.

> 'A good laugh and a long sleep are
> the best cures in the doctor's book.'
> —*Irish proverb*

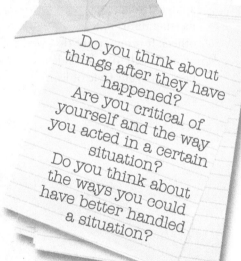

Do you think about things after they have happened? Are you critical of yourself and the way you acted in a certain situation? Do you think about the ways you could have better handled a situation?

Independent study

Developing independent study skills is a major requirement of university life. Consequently, establishing a sound study routine outside of your lecture and tutorial contact hours is vital to achieving your learning goals. A university study workload will be similar to a full-time job, even though your timetable will only show formal, regular lectures and tutorial times.

Locate your topic study plan, then clearly plan your independent study routine.

Independent study routines will vary for each student, but will encompass reading, researching, writing, reviewing, applying your skills and knowledge, meeting tutors and collaborating with others. It is important that you find an approach to independent study which best suits your style of learning.

What does 'independent study' mean to you?

Consider the following words and phrases, and identify those which describe how you would manage your independent study.

Circle the words/phrases which apply to you. Ask yourself: Would I . . .

Work on my own?

Ask for help?

Have no structure?

Plan goals and steps?

Feel stressed?

Manage my own learning?

Work with others?

Be uncertain?

Feel empowered?

Regard it as free time?

Explore my learning?

Want less help?

Belong to a study group?

Take responsibility?

Wait for others to lead?

What insight do these questions reveal to you about your learning approach?

How do your answers match with what you learned about yourself earlier in the chapter?

Underline the questions which demonstrate self-discipline and independent learning.

Active learners are:

- enthusiastic
- involved
- empowered
- self-directed
- capable
- collaborative
- creative.

Are you an active learner?

Independent study encompasses:

- motivating yourself to learn
- organising your own time
- working on your own, outside of contact hours
- planning your assignments
- reflecting continually on your learning progress
- reading prescribed texts and engaging in prescribed learning activities
- undertaking research
- writing (for example, notes, assignments, assessments, presentations)
- reviewing your lecture notes, tutorial notes, team work, and so on
- practising your skills and knowledge (for example, completing a practice exam, debating with others)
- collaborating with others
- working in study groups
- seeking help
- meeting tutors and lecturers
- asking questions
- accessing specialist support, such as Liaison Librarians
- discussing new learning
- clarifying your ideas
- sharing resources.

The challenge is to be open and receptive to your learning and employ a range of strategies. You need to be flexible and adapt to new ways of doing things. Other students may have tried out a strategy which works for them; it may be worth trying this for yourself. Take advantage of the many opportunities available at university to explore and research, to grow your knowledge and understanding, and to expand your horizons.

Always remember to be an active, independent learner!

As an active learner, you will take responsibility for your own learning by employing a range of strategies for your independent study.

Affirm your independent study skills by ticking the boxes below that apply to you now and then reviewing your progress at the end of semester one.

Characteristics	Now	End of semester one
I am autonomous		
> I am able to work alone		
> I understand my own learning style		
> I know where I prefer to study		
> I choose when to work with others		
> I know when and where to seek assistance		
I am self-motivated		
> I am able to organise my own time		
> I can plan my study routine		
> I am able to maintain focus		
> I am open-minded		
> I accept challenges		
> I prepare well		
I am respectful		
> I demonstrate inclusiveness to all		
> I value others		
> I am ethical		

continues

Characteristics	Now	End of semester one
I am able to reflect		
> I monitor my learning		
> I can give feedback		
> I acknowledge and consider feedback		
I set goals		
> I maintain my focus ·		
> I develop realistic and achievable goals		
> I review my goals		
I am a team player		
> I collaborate with others		
> I contribute to team goals		
> I facilitate the achievement of group goals		
> I am able to share in leading discussions		
> I encourage others		
> I participate in study groups		
I engage with my learning		
> I am punctual		
> I am actively involved		
> I am up to date with all aspects of study		
> I ask questions		
> I share my learning		
> I enjoy learning		
I am a critical thinker		
> I can absorb and apply new knowledge		
> I can analyse and evaluate new learning		
> I can develop a hypothesis and investigate it further		

Independent study can be a journey of self-discovery as you reflect on your progress, checking off your goals as you reach them and acknowledging your achievements. This experience can be extremely rewarding as long as you commit to both the ups and downs of the journey. Learning to study independently will enable you to develop lifelong learning skills and empower you in your future endeavours.

Use natural lighting when possible. Turn off the lights when you are not in the room.

Teamwork

Learning at university gives you the opportunity to work with other students in a variety of ways. Cooperating on assessment tasks, forming study groups, delivering oral presentations and participating in online discussions are just a few examples of collaborative teamwork. Working with others whose culture, life experiences and perspectives are different from your own broadens your outlook and is a positive strategy to enhance your learning. Interacting adds richness which you cannot achieve in the same way on your own.

Teamwork will increase your ability to think critically and, together with your independent study, will give you a more holistic and enriched understanding of a subject. As with independent study, the purposes of team work are to:

> motivate yourself and other team members
> organise and manage your time around others
> collectively plan your team assignment routine

- acknowledge the contribution of each individual
- contribute to the collective knowledge of the team
- accept responsibility with equality and fairness
- undertake collaborative research
- share resources, including your own notes, for the benefit of the team goal
- support each other
- seek help from tutors and lecturers
- reflect as a team on your progress
- acknowledge team achievements.

Teamwork involves cooperation and a willingness to acknowledge the different skills and talents of others, which in a team setting can be shared for the benefit of all. These roles may include specialist skills in planning, leading, doing, thinking, researching, IT and speaking, all of which contribute to the effectiveness of the whole team (see Figure 1.4).

The team roles are not exclusive to one individual and may in fact be shared across a number of members. What *is* important is the way in which the team manages the different roles and dynamics.

Teams move through a number of different stages whilst the members learn to work effectively with one another. Bruce Tuckman (1965) developed a theory to explain team formation which helps us understand the way teams operate. He identified four stages which characterise team development: forming, storming, norming and performing. (A fifth stage, grieving, was added later.) The team may fluctuate between the first two stages as they learn about each other and agree on the team roles. The duration of these stages will depend on how often the team meets and over what period of time – for example, over a semester as opposed to a week. As team members become more comfortable with each other and recognise the value of the contributions made by each, the team will gradually progress into the third and fourth stages.

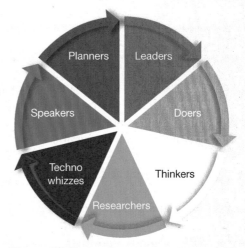

Figure 1.4 Team roles

Table 1.6 Overview of Tuckman's theory of team formation

Stage	Characteristics of each stage of team formation
FORMING	❭ get to know each other ❭ interact politely ❭ someone takes a lead ❭ negotiate a plan of action ❭ identify members' skills
STORMING	❭ more familiar with one another ❭ begin to speak out more freely ❭ debate proposed plans ❭ some want to act, while others need to think ❭ conflict may arise
NORMING	❭ begin to cooperate more effectively as a team ❭ listen to each other ❭ negotiate and find consensus ❭ resolve conflicts
PERFORMING	❭ work collaboratively to achieve team goals ❭ solve problems ❭ have clear roles ❭ have clear responsibilities ❭ function well as a team

Understanding the dynamics of a team and how it operates will enable you to be an effective team member and make the most of the learning opportunity.

At university you will frequently be required to work collaboratively with others in a team. Having an awareness of common team dynamics and challenges will allow you to identify the strengths and weaknesses of a team and develop strategies to develop and improve team skills. Go to the Mind Tools link (www.mindtools.com/pages/article/newLDR_86.htm) to complete a self-assessment which will help you and your team identify common team dynamics and challenges. As you do this, consider your previous team experiences. Alternatively, you may like to refer back to this self-assessment once you have begun to work in a team in your university study, in order to evaluate and appreciate the team roles.

Effective team guidelines

- Show trust and respect.
- Communicate openly and maintain confidentiality within the team.
- Cooperate and share.
- Express ideas and opinions.
- Set boundaries.
- Acknowledge that conflict is normal.
- Reach decisions by consensus.
- Value one another's skills.

Go to http://www.celt.iastate.edu/teaching/teaching-format/team-based-learning/ and scroll down the page to 'Student Commentary on Team-Based Learning in Clinical Pathology'. Watch the video, then answer the following questions.

1. What were some of the preconceived ideas which the three students identified as limitations of team work?
2. What were the positive outcomes that emerged from the team experience?
3. What is the final comment?
4. Why is this statement relevant to you within the university environment? This is a reflective question. It is expected that the answer will incorporate your thoughts and feelings about team-based learning as an active learner.

Strategies to support your learning within academic environments

Active listening

Within the different university environments you will need to employ effective listening skills. However, active listening is much more than just hearing what is said. A lecturer can deliver the information, but unless you get involved and process what you have heard, it will not make sense and you will not be able to remember it later: this is *passive* listening. In contrast, an *active* listener focuses on what is being said, listens carefully, rephrases, asks questions and takes notes. This is a dynamic two-way process which engages both the listener (who receives, processes and reacts to the information) and the speaker (who delivers, listens and responds). (See Figure 1.5.)

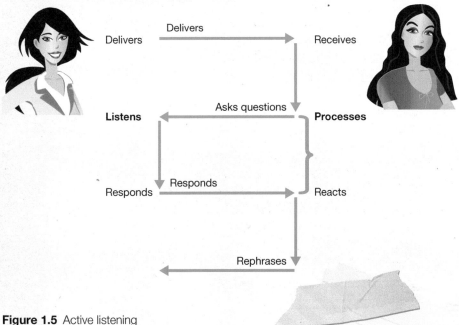

Figure 1.5 Active listening

To be an active listener, focus on:
> *what* is being said
> *how* it is being said
> the *context* in which it is being said.

As you listen, you focus your attention, anticipate content, and consider how it is said and the context in which it is being said. You will then be able to make connections between what you already know and what you are learning and to analyse this new information.

What strategies can you think of to develop your active listening skills?

Active listening will improve your memory and recall, build your confidence, and empower you to discuss, debate, question, explore, and give and receive feedback. It is vital for successfully negotiating academic environments, as well as being an important life skill.

Strategies for active listening

- Prepare to listen: bring notebook and pen, sit where you can hear, see and minimise distractions.
- Be respectful: focus on the person communicating.
- Digest new information by connecting to what you already know.
- Be observant: look for cues from the speaker to enhance meaning (such as tone, vocabulary, emphasis).
- Engage with the speaker: use non-verbal communication to demonstrate interest (for example, nodding, eye contact, leaning forward).
- Provide feedback: rephrase the speaker's main ideas. (By paraphrasing the main ideas, you are reinforcing the new information and are more likely to absorb it into your long-term memory.)
- Ask questions and interact as requested by the speaker.
- Listen objectively and keep an open mind.
- Be prepared to express an opinion and offer an explanation. This allows you to analyse the new information.
- Use appropriate language to demonstrate respect and inclusiveness.

Note taking

Taking notes in lectures, tutorials or group sessions, in conjunction with active listening skills, is a proven way of effectively organising information and remembering what is learnt. Recording information visually, as well as hearing it, further reinforces your ability to understand, make connections and recall that information.

Note taking also allows you to better focus your attention on the topic and concentrate on what is being said. The more you listen, take notes and concentrate, the more easily you will understand and make connections between your acquired knowledge and the new information. In the long term, taking notes as you actively listen is an efficient strategy which provides you with an additional source of information for assignments and exams revision.

Note taking

- develops your understanding of the topic
- requires you to listen actively
- aids your recall
- provides resources for assignment and exam revision.

The more strategies you actively employ in your learning, the greater your chances of success!

Note-taking strategies

Note taking is an academic skill which requires practice. It involves being able to successfully record the key information as you actively listen. You may face challenges as you learn this skill. You might find that it is difficult to keep up with the speaker's pace; that you don't understand the main points; that you do not immediately see the connection between examples given and the content; and, most frustratingly, that you cannot decipher your own notes. In order to manage these challenges, remember to listen actively, involve yourself in understanding what is being said and use the following strategies to guide your note taking:

> Preview readings to become familiar with terms and ideas.
> Listen for the main points and record key words.
> Keep your notes short and to the point.
> Use a form of abbreviation and punctuation which you will understand later.
> Condense the information as much as possible without losing meaning.
> Write in your own words where possible.
> Write clearly so you can interpret your handwriting later.
> Use the lecturer's pauses to add missed information.

Use your own words whenever possible.

Effective note-taking habits

- Be prepared with pen, paper, notebook, laptop or device.
- Start with a fresh page for each lecture or day, for easy reference.
- Record the topic and name of the presenter.
- Include the date and number every page.
- Select a note-taking format which suits you.
  - Leave a wide margin so that you can annotate your notes.
  - Write on one side of the page only; this leaves space for reviewing notes or adding more information.
  - Annotate handouts if provided.
- Correctly record all references.
- Structure your notes.

There are many different ways of recording information. Find a method of note taking that best suits your learning style. You will benefit from clear and logical notes. For more information on note taking refer to Chapter 3. Refining your note-taking skills will require practice. If you missed any information during a lecture or you wish to review your notes from a lecture, use the lectures, vodcasts or podcasts where these have been made available on FLO.

activity 1.13

Choose an online lecture from FLO to practise your active listening and note-taking skills.

Listen to the recording three times.

1. The first time, just listen!
2. Listen again and take notes.
3. Review your notes to confirm that they make sense.
4. Finally, listen again to clarify that your notes are accurate.

Reflect

When you are thinking reflectively, you are considering what has happened, how it happened and how you might have reacted differently. Making a conscious decision to reflect on your thoughts and feelings around a situation will give you insight into yourself and allow you to evaluate and improve your own performance. At university, thinking about your learning, considering what has happened, why it has happened, and how it impacts you as a learner is known as *reflection*. This is an invaluable active learning skill.

To reflect means to review and consider events, but it is much more than just listing what has happened. In reflecting you explore your feelings, form opinions, make judgements and evaluate your own performance in an active and positive way.

Reflecting empowers you to:

- analyse
- evaluate
- monitor your learning journey
- identify areas for improvement
- recognise your strengths
- select strategies that suit your learning style
- implement these strategies successfully
- experiment
- increase your self-awareness
- plan for the future
- discover opportunities
- challenge and question ideas.

Levels of reflection

You might have kept a diary in the past, or you may keep one still – perhaps in the form of a blog or a reflective journal. The value of any of these forms is that they:

> record events
> help you make sense of things
> build up an understanding of events over time
> allow you to write freely.

However, in order to be useful in academic writing and study, a diary needs to do more than this. It needs to track how a person learns from experience, to enable them to reflect upon experience and develop their awareness of the way they learn, so helping them to place it in a wider context. Good quality reflection needs to demonstrate depth and not just present the surface when describing events. This is of course a quality that is important in all academic writing.

Moving up through the levels

Hatton and Smith (1995) attribute many of our current ideas about reflection to John Dewey (writing in the first half of the twentieth century), who saw the link between reflection and problem-solving, a key skill in academic study. Hatton and Smith carried out research on reflection in teacher education and developed a framework to describe reflective writing which moves from pure description to the writer conducting a dialogue with the self and finally standing back from events to put them in a broader context. They define the framework, with its four stages, as follows:

1. descriptive writing (a straightforward account of events)
2. descriptive reflection (an account with reasons, justifications and explanations for events)
3. dialogic reflection (the writer begins to stand back from the account and analyse it)
4. critical reflection (the writer puts their account into a broader perspective).

Examples of reflection

Look at these examples that all describe the same situation.

1. Last week was the start of the new term. I have lectures on Mondays, Tuesdays and Thursdays until the end of the semester. That gives me a lot of free time, which is great. It also means I can carry on with my part-time job.

2. Last week was the start of the new term. I have lectures on Mondays, Tuesdays and Thursdays until the end of the semester. That gives me a lot of free time, which is great. It also means I can carry on with my part-time job but I will have to be very organised in the way I manage my time.

3. Last week was the start of the new term. I have lectures on Mondays, Tuesdays and Thursdays until the end of the semester. That gives me a lot of free time, which is great. It also means I can carry on with my part-time job but I will have to be very organised in the way I manage my time. I don't want to end up in the same situation as last year, when I was constantly running to stand still and always handing in work at the last minute. It really put me under pressure and made me realise the value of planning ahead.

In Example 1, the writer simply describes a situation (starting a new term, their timetable). In Example 2, they mention part-time work and the need to be organised. In Example 3, they are exploring the impact of something and resolving to do better. They are moving through the first three of the four stages of reflection mentioned earlier.

The language of reflection

As we said in the introduction to this chapter, there is a freedom in writing reflectively that you do not normally receive in academic writing. 'I' is allowed, along with contractions, exclamation marks, stray thoughts and unfinished sentences. In the examples given above the writer uses 'I', talks about their feelings ('great', 'put me under pressure') and uses far more casual language than you would normally see in academic writing where 'don't' is unacceptable and 'running to stand still' would be seen as inappropriate. In academic writing, it is important to avoid using emotive language and to be cautious in your use of language. While you can allow yourself to write in a way that may come more naturally to you, make sure you do not just put down random thoughts that you cannot make any sense of later on.

The need for structure

Reflective writing in an academic context must still be thorough and systematic and aim for depth of understanding and analysis. As a writer you will have more control over the subject matter, but you need to make sure that you follow certain academic standards to produce good quality reflective writing. This means you must try to:

> support the points you make with examples drawn from your experience
> explore the implications and consequences of your actions
> consider different perspectives on the events you write about.

That way you will demonstrate your ability to analyse, evaluate and synthesise – and so show that you are able to use the higher order of intellectual skills expected in academic study.

Even though there are no real rules for *what* to write, you do need to think about *how* to express your thoughts. Hatton and Smith's research (1995) found that the following kind of language helped writers develop their skill at reflecting:

'This was quite possibly due to ... Alternatively, ...'

'The problem here, I believe, was the fact that ...'

'On the one hand, ... yet on the other ...'

'In thinking back, ... On reflection ...'

If you think about these words you will see that the writer(s) are considering:

> reasons for an event
> alternative solutions
> different points of view
> problems that were caused.

In addition, they are demonstrating the ability to analyse and evaluate.

Phrases to encourage reflection

Think of other phrases that you could use to develop your skills of reflection:

_____

_____

_____

_____

Judging the quality of reflective writing

One of the problem areas in reflective writing is how and whether to assess it. Since it is a very personal way of writing standard methods of assessment are less suitable. However it *is* possible to look for certain characteristics and to try to develop them in your own writing. Examples of these characteristics are that the writing:

> considers time-frames
> is aware of uncertainties and the relative nature of things
> speculates on the consequences of actions
> thinks about change
> focuses on one or two events that it then explores in depth
> relates events to personal development.

Here are three examples for you to compare. Each account is of the same event (the writer's experience of group work).

Example A

Last week was the group presentation for our project. It went fairly well, we passed. Some of the group had really not pulled their weight; they never turned up to meetings or replied to their emails. I remember our lecturer covered group work at the beginning of the term, when she handed out the assignment. We did a questionnaire and I came out as the sort that always gets things done in the end, which is more than you can say for some of the others in my group. Still, maybe the next time I have to do group work I'll be luckier.

Example B

Last week I took part in a group presentation about the project we have been doing all this term. It went fairly well, we passed and were given some really useful feedback. Some of the group had not contributed much over the term, they rarely turned up to meetings or replied to emails. That meant that we hardly ever had everyone there at the same time so it was very difficult to agree the different jobs that had to be done, who should do them and in what order.

I remember our lecturer covered group work at the beginning of the term, when she handed out the assignment. We talked about what makes an effective team, the stages you have to go through, team roles and team types. We completed a questionnaire and I was classified as the sort that always gets things done in the end. I was pleased about that, I think that is one of the types you really need in a team and I like to think of myself as cooperative and hardworking, which is more than you can say for some of the others in my group. Still, maybe the next time I have to do group work I'll be luckier or I might insist we draw up some ground rules before the first meeting.

Example C

Last week I took part in a group presentation about the project we have been doing all this term. It went fairly well, we passed and were given some really useful feedback. It said that we spoke well, kept to time and used very effective computer visuals. However it marked us down on evidence of working as a team. Some of the group had not contributed much over the term, they rarely turned up to meetings or replied to emails. That meant that we hardly ever had everyone there at the same time so it was very difficult to agree the different jobs that had to be done, who should do them and in what order. It meant that some of us had to do far more than our fair share. Looking back on it now, we should have tried to do something about it earlier.

I remember our lecturer covered group work at the beginning of the term, when she handed out the assignment. We talked about what makes an effective team, the stages you have to go through, team roles and team types. We discussed how you can build up a team and how you can ruin a team, that was very helpful. We completed a questionnaire and I was classified as the sort that always gets things done in the end. I was pleased about that, I think that is one of the types you really need in a team (as well as in any future employment) and I like to think of myself as cooperative and hardworking, which is more than you can say for some of the others in my group. Still, maybe the next time I have to do group work I'll be luckier or I might insist we draw up some ground rules before the first meeting. I mustn't pretend I was perfect though – I did skip a few meetings without warning anyone. I'll certainly make sure I don't behave like that again, it shows a lack of respect. On balance, I would say this was a useful exercise to go through, but the problem with it was that we were not all fully committed as a team.

The areas that have been highlighted show examples of some of the characteristics of reflective writing mentioned above. Account B has more reflection than A, and C has more reflection than B.

> It is not sufficient simply to have an experience in order to learn. Without reflecting upon this experience it may quickly be forgotten, or its learning potential lost. It is from the feelings and thoughts emerging from this reflection that generalisations or concepts can be generated. And it is generalisations that allow new situations to be tackled effectively.
> —(Gibbs, 1998, p. 9)

Be honest and genuine with yourself when you reflect.

Actively reflect

The following six steps provide you with a guide to active reflection.

1. Briefly outline the context.

   'Today we had to work in groups to summarise Chapter 7.'

2. Brainstorm your thoughts, feelings, beliefs, assumptions and attitudes.

   'I felt uncomfortable today. I wonder why I felt reluctant to be involved?'

3. Analyse these thoughts, feelings, beliefs and assumptions.

   'Perhaps I felt uncomfortable because I haven't worked with these students before and I didn't know how we would all work together as a group.'

4. Evaluate your reaction.

   'Looking back, I realise I made assumptions about the students in my group. As we started talking I discovered that everyone was able to contribute something, even me! Surprising, considering my first impressions.'

5. Consider what was good and what went well.

   'I enjoyed listening to the discussion and felt more comfortable about contributing.'

6. Identify areas for improvement and select strategies to address the change.

   'Maybe I need to pause before jumping to conclusions. I guess it takes time for everyone to feel relaxed and work together. Hmm! Perhaps I could review Tuckman's model (1965) of group roles. I'll have to keep this in mind for next time.'

Active learners make conscious decisions to continually reflect on their learning.

Active reflection steps

1. Briefly outline the context.
2. Brainstorm your thoughts, feelings, beliefs, assumptions and attitudes.
3. Analyse these thoughts, feelings, beliefs and assumptions.
4. Evaluate your reaction.
5. Consider what was good and what went well.
6. Identify areas for improvement and select strategies to address the change.

Critical thinking

Critical thinking is a highly valued academic skill. It takes time and practice to develop. Active listening and note taking are the basis upon which you can enrich your understanding and begin to build your capacity to think critically.

Thinking involves being able to: consider, predict, presume, deduce, believe, conclude and reflect.

Thinking *critically* involves all these abilities, plus being able to diagnose, interpret, evaluate, explain, probe, analyse and synthesise.

Critical thinking is a higher level of thinking which requires an active commitment to practise and refine to an academic standard. Every aspect of your academic journey will involve thinking critically. Consequently, it is crucial that you make a conscientious decision to approach *all* your learning in this way. The ability to think critically involves being able to:

> compare both sides of an argument
> analyse an issue from different perspectives
> examine bias
> evaluate underlying assumptions
> determine whether a conclusion is justified
> formulate a point of view
> appraise a model or theory
> organise and construct information.

The Active Learning Approach will support your endeavours to become a critical thinker. Engage in all aspects of your learning, ask questions, interact in tutorials, participate in study groups where you can discuss and debate, talk to your lecturer and tutor, and read widely. This commitment to your learning will stimulate your desire to know more in order to deepen your understanding, and challenge your own and others' ideas. Using *what*, *when*, *where*, *how* and *why* questions will get you started. These questions will focus your attention and prompt you to think on a deeper level using higher-order thinking skills.

Consider what skills you will need to think critically.

Chapter summary

The university experience is unique. It is an academic environment which has its own demands and challenges. Developing the skills of active listening, note taking and critical thinking will greatly assist you to negotiate these environments. If you build on your previous experiences, anticipate and actively engage in new learning opportunities, you will realise the attainment of your personal goals, broaden your horizons and be open to future possibilities.

You are embarking on a learning journey that will be full of surprises, challenges and opportunities. Active learning is about *you*; it is a choice that you make that will enable you to:

> identify and use learning strategies that suit your style of learning
> develop a study routine
> manage your stress effectively
> reflect and gain new insights
> maintain focus and motivation.

Each of these skills will empower you to be an effective lifelong learner. Enjoy the journey!

Summary activities

1. Describe the differences between the vocational college/school and university learning environment and learning approach.
2. What positive actions can you take to adapt to university?
3. How you will maximise your learning in independent study?
4. How will you participate in an effective team?

Reflection

How will you successfully negotiate your academic learning environments?

> Which aspects do you feel confident about?
> What aspects challenge you?
> What strategies will you use in each of the learning environments?

Photo credits

12 © ivylingpy/Shutterstock; **13** © Monkey Business Images/Shutterstock; **41** © Gemenacom/Shutterstock; **64** © Rob Wilson/Shutterstock.

2 Get it Write!

Structure your writing

At university you will gain experience using a variety of writing styles. You may initially feel uncomfortable with writing in an academic style, but as you become more familiar with the different formats you will build confidence. These are skills that you may or may not have developed well in the past but they are essential to academic writing. Knowing the basic structures of writing, including how to structure paragraphs (with introductory, supporting and concluding sentences) and how to link ideas logically throughout a piece of writing, will provide you with the foundation for all forms of writing, particularly in academia.

Overview of writing structures

Creating sentences

The purpose of a sentence is to allow the writer to communicate facts and information, and to express ideas and thoughts clearly and without ambiguity. To do this, you must form your sentences so that they state your meaning in a coherent and precise manner. An unstructured sentence causes confusion and loses its meaning.

In its simplest form, a sentence is composed of a selection of words that contain at least a subject (what the sentence is about) and a verb (what is happening). In academia, a particular standard of writing is expected. This is because you will need to convey more complex ideas, thoughts and theories, which cannot be expressed in simple sentences. As you develop your writing skills, you will discover how to express your ideas creatively. This topic is discussed in detail in Chapter 3.

Every sentence:
> contains at least one noun and one verb
> is straightforward and unambiguous
> begins with a capital letter
> ends with a full stop (or question mark)
> includes correct punctuation. (If you are unsure, check.)

Kinds of sentences

In addition to the six patterns of a simple sentence, there are four kinds of sentences in English. We form the different kinds by combining dependent and independent clauses in different patterns.

Simple sentences

A simple sentence is one independent clause.

```
┌──────────────────────── independent clause ────────────────────────┐
```
> A sports teacher invented the game of basketball about 100 years ago.

Compound sentences

A compound sentence is two independent clauses connected in one of three ways.

> ⎡——————— independent clause ———————⎤
> The game of basketball was invented in the United States, **but**
>
> ⎡——— independent clause ———⎤
> it is now popular all over the world.

> ⎡——————— independent clause ———————⎤
> Basketball was invented in the United States; **however,**
>
> ⎡——— independent clause ———⎤
> it is now popular all over the world.

> ⎡——————— independent clause ———————⎤ ⎡——————— independent clause ———————⎤
> Basketball was invented in the United States; it is now popular all over the world.

Complex sentences

A complex sentence is one independent clause and at least one dependent clause.

> ⎡——— independent clause ———⎤ ⎡——————— dependent clause ———————⎤
> A sports teacher invented the game because he wanted his students to have a sport
>
> ⎡——————— dependent clause ———————⎤
> that they could play indoors during the cold months of winter.

> ⎡——— independent clause ———⎤ ⎡——————— dependent clause ———————
> The first baskets were peach baskets, which were attached to the walls of the
>
> ⎡——————⎤
> school gymnasium.

Compound-complex sentences

A compound-complex sentence has at least two independent clauses and at least one dependent clause.

> ⎡——— independent clause ———⎤ ⎡——————— dependent clause ———————
> The first baskets were peach baskets, which were attached to the walls of the
>
> ⎡——————⎤ ⎡——————— independent clause ———————⎤
> school gymnasium, and the first basketballs were soccer balls.

Structuring paragraphs

The purpose of paragraphs is to organise and sequence ideas, convey meaning and engage the reader. Different ideas are expressed in each paragraph, and the paragraphs become the building blocks of writing which, when skilfully constructed, form longer and coherent pieces of writing.

Each paragraph contains a group of sentences linked by one idea:

The topic sentence	› Conveys the main idea of the paragraph
Supporting sentences	› Expand the main point
	› Offer explanations
	› Give examples/additional details
The concluding/linking sentence	› Summarises the paragraph
	› Provides a link to the next paragraph

The short paragraph below demonstrates complex sentence structure. It includes: a topic sentence, which introduces the main point of the paragraph; a supporting sentence, which further develops the main idea; and a concluding sentence, which restates the main point in a different way.

> *What is important to clarify is that there are differing ethical issues that occur for different health care disciplines with differing levels of complexity. For example, nurses may consider a client's privacy while undertaking a bed-bath as an important ethical issue, whereas a doctor may consider that the right time to give a client a diagnosis is an important ethical issue. As well as this, some ethical issues are of public concern and are discussed in the media, such as cloning or stem cell research. These issues are controversial and nurses may or may not be directly involved in this work. Other ethical issues do not necessarily attract public or media coverage. The day-to-day care that nurses provide can often be fraught with ethical concerns. Privacy, confidentiality, client choice, and even clinical interventions, such as hydration or performing a painful procedure, are all part of the nurse's professional and ethical domain. (McPherson & Stakenberg, 2012, p. 96)*

activity
2.1

Practise writing a paragraph which contains a topic sentence, supporting sentences and a concluding sentence, in response to the following statement:

Define what you think a nurse is.

Use biodegradable pens to reduce the production of plastic and landfill.

Writing guidelines

A variety of communication styles are used in academia: oral presentations; debates; reports; essays and case studies. The written forms differ significantly from oral forms of language. In conversation you have a greater opportunity to express yourself and give immediate feedback to clarify what you mean, or to restate your point. In writing, however, you must choose your words with greater care to convey your intended meaning to the reader. This is particularly important in academic writing, where a more formal and precise style of language is used.

Features of formal academic style

When developing a piece of writing for academic purposes, you will choose vocabulary and construct sentences that have a formal tone without using personal pronouns, contractions and colloquial language (see Figure 2.1).

Personal pronoun

Contraction

Informal	Formal
We tested our hypothesis by performing a blind trial experiment. We weren't able to put our request into the ethics committee until late April, which meant we were behind the eight ball.	The hypothesis was tested using a blind trial experiment. The request was not lodged with the ethics committee until late April, which put the project behind schedule.

Colloquialism

Figure 2.1 Writing styles

Experiment with vocabulary and use a dictionary to assist you in determining word meaning. A thesaurus can be useful in expanding your vocabulary. However, any new words should be used in their correct context, whilst taking into account the subtle changes in word meanings. For example:

There was a medication calculation error.
There was a medication stuff-up.

In these examples the second sentence demonstrates an inappropriate choice of words that impairs the clarity and impact of the statement. The first sentence is exact and clear.

In academic writing select words and phrases that express your ideas in a clear and straightforward way, without the use of **slang** or **idiom**. For example:

The decision was made <u>at the eleventh hour</u>.
We <u>had a go</u> at putting together a questionnaire.

These sentences which contain idioms illustrate an inappropriate choice of vocabulary for an academic context.

It is essential to select enough words to express your meaning without being **verbose**. For example:

If you make use of too many unnecessary, complex words and phrases with an emphasis on adjectives, which are words to describe a noun, you will extensively lengthen the sentence, obscure the meaning, and perplex the reader who is trying to comprehend and appreciate what you are endeavouring to get across.

This could be written more simply. For example:

Using too many words reduces the meaning and clarity of the sentence.

You may use rhetorical questions. A rhetorical question is one that does not expect an answer. It is used to propose an idea or to provoke the reader to think. For example:

Is the sky blue?

Use rhetorical questions sparingly for impact and only to enhance your writing. Table 2.1 is an example of writing guidelines you may find useful.

Table 2.1 Samples from a style guide

	Not acceptable	Acceptable
Abbreviations Avoid where possible.	dept. uni. ph.	department university phone
Contractions Use the full words.	can't doesn't they're	cannot does not they are
Numbers Spell numbers one to nine.	1, 2, 3 . . .	One, two, three . . .
Inclusive language	man, woman, mankind	humankind people individual community
Use of adverbs and adjectives Too many may be seen as a value judgement.	The horrendous and tragic ramifications of the recent catastrophic world events are a reminder of humanity's inability to curb its selfish, greedy desires.	Recent world events are a reminder of the impacts of humanity on the planet.

Gender, religion, nationality, racial groups, age, and physical or mental characteristics should only be referred to if the information is relevant to what you are writing. If these characteristics are irrelevant, then select non-specific vocabulary in their place.

Active/passive voice

These terms are opposites and refer to a particular structure of writing. The tone of the sentence can change depending on the choice of passive or active voice.

Grammar checkers almost always mark passive sentences as questionable. This does not always mean that you should rewrite them in the active voice. Sometimes the passive voice is more appropriate. You will have to decide if your passive sentences are appropriate.

Sentences are in either the active or the passive voice. In active sentences, the subject *performs* the action of the verb. We want to emphasise the performer of the action, so we put the subject in front of the verb.

> **Michelangelo painted** the ceiling of the Sistine Chapel.

In passive sentences, the subject receives the action of the verb. We want to emphasise what happened, not who did it. The performer of the action is either unknown or unimportant, so the performer goes after the verb or is not mentioned at all.

> **Our house was painted** last year.

Passive verb forms

We form the passive voice with various tenses of *be* + a past participle.

SIMPLE TENSES		PERFECT TENSES	
Present	It **is written**	Present perfect	It **has been written**
Past	It **was written**	Past perfect	It **had been written**
Future	It **will be written** It **is going to be written**	Future perfect	It **will have been written**
PROGRESSIVE TENSES			
Present	It **is being written**		
Past	It **was being written**		

An object (direct or indirect) of an active sentence becomes the subject of a passive sentence. The subject of an active sentence becomes a phrase beginning with *by* or disappears entirely.

ACTIVE SENTENCES	PASSIVE SENTENCES
┌───O───┐ > Maria **wrote** the best essay.	┌───S───┐ > The best essay **was written** *by Maria.*
┌──O──┐ > People **speak** Portuguese in Brazil.	┌──S──┐ > Portuguese **is spoken** in Brazil (*by people*).[1]
┌─O─┐ > Someone **stole** my car yesterday.	┌─S─┐ > My car **was stolen** yesterday (*by someone*).[2]

[1] It was unnecessary to say *by people*, so it was omitted.
[2] It was unknown who stole my car, so *by someone* was omitted.

Both the direct object and the indirect object of an active sentence can become the subject of a passive sentence.

ACTIVE SENTENCES	PASSIVE SENTENCES
⟩ My fiancé gave me **this ring**. ⌐ DO ¬	⟩ **This ring** was given to me by my fiancé. ⌐ S ¬
⟩ My fiancé gave **me** this ring. IO	⟩ **I** was given this ring by my fiancé. S

You can make passive sentences only from transitive verbs because only transitive verbs can have objects. Therefore, you cannot write passive sentences with verbs such as *seem*, *happen*, *live*, *go*, *fall*, or *die*. For example, you cannot say *He was died* because *die* is an intransitive verb. You have to use *kill* to make a passive sentence: *He was killed*.

To make a passive sentence negative, put *not* after the first helping verb.

⟩ Bananas **are** *not* **grown** in Alaska.
⟩ This book **has** *not* **been translated** into English yet.
⟩ Fish **should** *not* **be overcooked**.

ACTIVE VOICE	PASSIVE VOICE
Present tenses	
⟩ Most people in the United States **eat** meat.	⟩ Meat **is eaten** by most people in the United States.
⟩ However, many Americans **are** now **eating** fish.	⟩ However, fish **is** now **being eaten** by many Americans.
⟩ People living near the sea **have** always **eaten** fish.	⟩ Fish **has** always **been eaten** by people living near the sea.
Past tenses	
⟩ Someone **painted** our house before we moved in.	⟩ Our house **was painted** before we moved in.
⟩ The painters **were** still **painting** it on the day we moved in.	⟩ It **was** still **being painted** on the day we moved in.
⟩ No one **had painted** it for many years.	⟩ It **hadn't been painted** for many years.

ACTIVE VOICE	PASSIVE VOICE
Future tenses	
Our two daughters **will share** the largest bedroom.	The largest bedroom **will be shared** by our two daughters.
We **are going to organise** the kitchen first.	The kitchen **is going to be organised** first.
By tomorrow night, we **will have put** everything in its proper place.	By tomorrow night, everything **will have been put** in its proper place.
Modals	
Present We **should send** change-of-address cards to our friends.	Change-of-address cards **should be sent** to our friends.
Past We **should have sent** them before we moved.	They **should have been sent** before we moved.
Infinitives	
Present Our neighbours **plan to welcome** us with a neighbourhood barbecue party.	We **hope to be welcomed** with a neighbourhood barbecue party.
Gerunds	
Present I look forward to someone **offering** me a job.	I look forward to **being offered** a job.

The use of either passive or active voice changes the meaning of your sentence. Using the passive voice, the noun performing the action is no longer the subject of the sentence. This can allow you to emphasise an important piece of information or to intentionally de-emphasise the noun.

At this point you may be wondering when to use the active or passive voice. The passive voice is often used in speech and writing. It is commonly used in textbooks, reports and in the media. Your topic details may suggest that you write in either the active or the passive voice depending on the purpose and formality of the writing. Reports are often written in the passive voice as they focus on a 'process' – that is, what happened, why it happened, how it happened. In report writing, *who* did the action is not always as important as *what* the action is. Compare these statements:

A questionnaire was developed . . .
I developed a questionnaire . . .

The first statement is the appropriate choice. In a report format, it is not important who developed the questionnaire; the significant fact is that a questionnaire was developed.

In a report, the use of the passive voice expresses a more formal, objective tone.

'It was revealed . . .'
'The methodology was chosen by the research team.'

Overusing the passive voice may create a less interesting piece of writing. Conversely, even if you are required to use the active voice, the occasional use of the passive voice can add emphasis, variety and interest to your writing. The key is to find the right balance to suit your purpose.

Active and Passive Voice

To create the active voice, ask 'who is doing it' and state this at the start of the sentence and then ask 'what are they doing' and put that in too.

Passive: Pain was felt by the patient.
Active: (who?) The patient (what?) felt pain.

The active sentence is really useful because it becomes easier to add in extra information, such as when it occurs, where it occurs, how it is done, who specifically does it, etc.

Passive: An occasional sharp shooting pain in the sides of the knee was felt by some of the patients in the study.
Active: Some patients in the study occasionally felt a sharp shooting pain in the sides of the knee.

Transform these passive sentences into the active voice

1. The medication was administered by the nurse.

   _____

   _____

2. To dress the wound, a sterile container, bandages, and scissors are used by the nurse.

   _____

   _____

3. Checking the chart, assessing the patient, verifying the last administration, and asking permission from the patient is needed by the nurse.

_____

_____

_____

4. The pathophysiology exam was failed by most students who struggled to complete their degree.

_____

_____

_____

5. The man was caught by the night duty nurse with no pants on.

_____

_____

Nominalisation

Nominalisation is often used in academic writing to present an authoritative and objective tone. It is a grammatical term used to describe the process of constructing sentences where the emphasis is on the nouns, rather than on the description of actions (verbs) or a clause. It occurs when you turn a verb or clause into a noun (naming word).

> During the lecture and tutorial we discussed nursing issues.
>
> *Verb*

The sentence above focuses on the use of the verb 'discuss'. The sentence below changes the verb 'discussed' into the noun 'discussion'.

> The tutorial discussion was about nursing issues.
>
> *Noun*

> The nurse who catheterises a patient must use special preparation techniques.
>
> *Verb*

In the second example, the focus is on catheterisation rather than the nurse doing it.

Catheterisation requires special preparation techniques.

      Noun

Nominalisation is a useful tool for ensuring that you do not lose the power of your writing through using too many words, but overusing it can result in a piece of writing that is difficult to read and understand. Use nominalisation to maximise the impact and quality of your writing.

Tentative statements

These are carefully worded, cautious statements used to qualify an assertion. Tentative statements are used in preference to making generalisations or extravagant claims. Whilst the scope of your topic will limit your research, offering a tentative statement can be used as a strategy to avoid making unsubstantiated claims or statements. It allows you to maintain objectivity and present a rational analysis.

It is widely believed that most flus are spread through coughing.

This statement is an unsupported claim; however, the example below supports the assertion with evidence.

Smith (2014) examined the relationship between airborne flu viruses and contracting the flu.

The first sentence below illustrates the use of a generalisation, whereas the second sentence uses carefully selected words to qualify the statement.

Coughing *passes* the flu to others.
Current research *suggests* a link between airborne flu virus and *indicates an increased likelihood* of catching the flu.

Using carefully selected verbs will help you to develop tentative statements.

Table 2.2 Verbs

Modal verbs	Verbs	Adverbs
Could, may, might	Appears, seems, suggests, indicates	Perhaps, possibly, likely, probably, may be, mostly

Showing confidence

You can show your degree of confidence in your claim by:

› showing caution in your claim though the use of hedges such as 'probable', 'might', 'may', 'possibly'

› showing confidence in your claim by using boosters such as 'definite', 'will', 'must', 'obviously', 'clearly'.

The sentence below is quite confident.

> *It is clear that schools need to introduce sport at a young age.*

Although your evidence may strongly support this argument, in academic writing the sentence may be expressed more cautiously with the use of a modal verb such as 'may':

> *It is clear that schools may need to introduce sport at a young age.*

You can use various verbs, adjectives or adverbs to show your degree of confidence as shown below:

Modal verbs	e.g. **will, may, might, could**
Apart from neuroanatomical differences, there may be differences in the amount of, or sensitivity to, hormones. (Martin *et al.*, 2007, p. 472)	
Modal adverbs	e.g. **certainly, definitely, probably, perhaps**
Abstract words are definitely first understood as adjectives. (Martin *et al.*, 2007, p. 415) The origin of language probably lies in the motor system of our brain. (Martin *et al.*, 2007, p. 450) Production has perhaps the greatest potential to clash with marketing. (Brassington and Pettitt, 2006, p. 26)	
Modal adjectives	e.g. **certain, definite**
The oligopoly creates a certain amount of interdependence between the key players, each of which is large enough for its actions to have a big impact on the market and on the behaviour of its competitors. (Brassington and Pettitt, 2006, p. 79)	
Signalling phrases	e.g. **it may be possible ..., it could be..., there is a chance that ..., in general**
As students are funding more of their studies there is a strong likelihood that they will be heavily in debt at the end of their degree. ... and it may be that the novel can be understood purely as entertainment ...	

Making relationships clear

Identify the words and phrases in the following sentences that show the writer's stance with regard to showing relationships.

> Ultimately, competitive edge is the name of the game.
>
> > (Brassington & Pettitt, 2006, p. 34)

> The evidence discussed so far indicates that cognitive ability, especially certain types of memory, declines with age ... They suggest that the decline reported is due to psychology not ageing per se. Similarly, Salthouse (1992; 1993; Craik & Salthouse, 2000) has argued that the elderly perform more poorly at cognitive tasks because they become slower at performing them.
>
> > (Martin et al., 2007, p. 491)

Whenever you are writing, make sure that you are clear about how parts of your text are related.

Showing the strength of your claim

You can show your attitude to the viewpoints, sources or the evidence that you have presented. The word that you choose in these two examples will alter the strength of the claim you are making about the relationship.

Compare

> *Research suggests that we possess at least four forms of memory.*
> > (Martin et al., 2007, p. 304)

with

> *Research proves that we possess at least four forms of memory.*
> > (Martin et al., 2007, p. 304)

Or

> *Nowadays the urinary symptoms are of a lower order.*

with

> *Nowadays the urinary symptoms appear to be of a lower order.*

As you can see, you can choose to use another word or phrase instead of the highlighted word, depending on how strongly you want to make your point. Remember always to support your points with evidence.

You could choose one of the following expressions:

X	indicates suggests proves	that ...

For example:

The evidence discussed so far indicates that cognitive ability, especially certain types of memory, declines with age. (Martin et al., 2007, p. 491)

In the following sentences, you have similar choices and you can choose one of the following phrases.

X	seems appears is believed is thought is presumed is assumed is known	to ...

For example:

The reported figures for incidence of disease are thought to represent 1 per cent of the true numbers.

Alternatively, when you are explicitly reporting the work of others, you have a choice of reporting verb:

X	believes suggests found argued discovered shows confirmed proved	that ...

For example:

Within the food sector, Bolton (1989) found that whereas coffee brands and convenience foods are very price elastic, certain types of fresh fruit and vegetables are price inelastic. (Brassington & Pettitt, 2006, p. 448)

Harré (2002) suggested that there were 12 uses of an experiment.
(Holden, 2008, p. 14)

In fact Lane (2001) argued that one of the ways science moves forward is by trying to solve disagreements between one set of findings and another set of findings that have been produced by a different method.
(Holden, 2008, p. 14)

In all cases, try changing the phrase and see what effect it has.

Demonstrating an objective view can be achieved through the use of a sentence that is prefaced by a tentative phrase:

It could be argued that . . .
The evidence suggests . . .
The results appear to demonstrate . . .
Research indicates . . .
It is most likely that . . .

As you research and begin to write for academic purposes, you will be drawing on the knowledge of past researchers and analysing what previous authors have written. This process requires an objective approach and an understanding that the body of knowledge on a topic is continually expanding. New ideas and understandings are constantly being proposed, refined and enhanced, and it is essential that you acknowledge that there will be other opinions which you have not been able to consider. The use of tentative statements will provide you with a strategy to develop a more objective response.

Contractions and abbreviations

Contractions and abbreviations are shortened words, which are not used in academic writing. Contractions include words such as *can't, won't, couldn't, he's* and *it's*, where a letter is replaced with an apostrophe. Abbreviations are words that are shortened to the first letters for convenience (*govt., dept., uni.*). Whilst these words are shortened in speech and informal writing, the full forms of the words are *always* used within academic writing.

Table 2.3 Common contractions and abbreviations

Full word	Contraction or abbreviation
can not (or cannot)	can't
will not	won't
could not	couldn't
he is	he's
it is	it's
government	govt.
department	dept.
university	uni.
business	bus.

The third person

When writing stories and narrative, the use of personal pronouns (the first person) is an accepted form of expression. 'I think that . . . ' However, the use of personal pronouns is generally not consistent with academic style. In academic writing, the use of the third person gives your writing a more formal and objective tone. 'It was found that . . . ' Using the third person puts you as the writer at a distance from what you are writing.

> *We* presented the results of *our* research to the ethics committee.

This sentence uses the personal pronouns 'we' and 'our', while the sentence below maintains an objective voice using the third person.

> The results of the research were presented to the ethics committee.

Table 2.4 First person and third person

First person	Third person
I, me, we, us	They, those, it, one, he, she, this, these Name the person involved or use titles – eg, Professor A. Smith, Minister for Finance, the committee, the authors

3rd and 1st Person Voice

To create the 3rd person voice, you need to remove words like *I, you, we, us, my,* and *our* from your sentences. This lets your ideas stand alone. Instead, you'll probably use sentence starters such as

it is ...   this situation causes ...   X writes ...   there will be ....

The 3rd person is objective and topic-centred. Professional writing is not about what you like, ate for lunch, or watched last night; rather, it is about communicating as a part of a professional or academic community. Consider these examples:

1st person: I don't like dealing with angry people.
3rd person: It is difficult dealing with angry people.

Ask yourself how would the 1st person statement above affect other's professional actions? The 1st person statement looks like a personal opinion. The 3rd person statement looks objective, and it points to a wider issue of dealing with difficult people, so it could be used as a reference in a paper that discusses communication problems, etc. The use of the 3rd person voice is a sign that you are trying to participate in body of scholarship around a topic.

Transform these 1st person sentences into the 3rd person

1. We think this is an interesting study.

_____

_____

2. I forgot the information quickly.

_____

_____

3. You should not be rude and you need to treat your patients with respect.

_____

_____

4. I was not sure that the higher grades were caused by better teaching.

_____

_____

5. I don't know if people read as many books as they used to.

_____

_____

Using the third person keeps the focus on the topic rather than on the person, making the tone impersonal, and presents a more objective perspective.

There are numerous resources, containing grammar explanations and activities, available from the university library and bookshop, as well as on the World Wide Web. The following five books are useful reference texts:

> Faigley, L. (2018). *The little Penguin handbook* (2nd ed.). Melbourne, VIC: Pearson Australia.
> Gillet, A. (2014). *Using English for academic purposes*. Retrieved from http://www.uefap.com/index.htm
> Gillett, A., Hammond, A., & Martala, M. (2009). *Inside tract to successful academic writing*. Harlow, England: Pearson Education Ltd.
> Oshima, A., & Hogue, A. (2006). *Writing academic English* (4th ed.). White Plains, NY: Pearson Longman.
> Purdue University. (2014). *The Purdue Online Writing Lab (OWL)*. Retrieved from https://owl.english.purdue.edu/owl/

Summary of academic style

These features of academic writing style help to maintain the focus of your writing on the topic rather than on opinion. They require you to make an informed decision about which words to use and to craft the words into well-constructed, meaningful, objective sentences. Writing in an academic style will take practice; therefore, rather than approaching it with apprehension, think of it as an opportunity to **hone** your writing skills, enhance your vocabulary, and express yourself in a clear and meaningful way.

Audience and purpose

There may be several purposes for writing in academia, some of which may include: to inform; persuade; report; investigate; compare and contrast; or discuss. Establishing the purpose of your writing is a vital step. Your writing style and language should relate to the purpose. To identify the purpose, look for clues in the assignment question. This will also enable you to select the appropriate tone and voice. If your purpose is to inform, you will include facts and substantiate your position. If your purpose is to report, you will include a description of what happened, when it happened how it happened, and make recommendations.

Important questions to ask yourself when identifying your purpose:

- Who is your audience? (Your lecturer, your peers?)
- What is the purpose of the writing? (To inform, to discuss . . .?)
- What format do you choose to suit the purpose? (If this has not been specified.)
- How will you present the information to engage the audience?
- What specific vocabulary and terminology should you use?

The next step is to establish what you will write about. This will be guided by your understanding of key instruction terms (see Table 2.5). It is important to acknowledge that your assignment or exam may contain more than one key action term or instruction. Consider whether you have responded equally to all instructions. Always provide supporting evidence to validate your answer (see Chapter 4).

Table 2.5 Key instruction terms

Analyse	Break down the topic to find the main ideas Investigate the components Show how they are related and why
Argue	Support or reject a position by presenting reasons and evidence in a rational manner
Assess	Consider the facts and link to theory Make a careful judgement on its validity Provide supporting evidence
Critique	Examine and analyse a point of view Make a judgement about the value
Define	Determine the parameters of your definition Describe clearly and concisely your understanding of the topic Support with evidence
Explain	Clarify and interpret Give a clear reason and justification for how and why something is

Table 2.5 Key instruction terms *continued*

Evaluate	Present the issue Consider all points of view Form your own opinion by drawing conclusions Support your position
Illustrate	Explain or clarify by using specific examples (graphs, pictures, table, visual concepts)
Interpret	Convey your understanding and reaction to a topic Explain why it has meaning or significance
Investigate	Examine the topic systematically Present and explore the facts Draw conclusions
Justify	Establish a position Develop a rationale to support your position
List/enumerate	Recount the points one by one
Outline	Provide an organised overview of the main points or general principles
Prove	Demonstrate with evidence that a theory or opinion is true
Relate	Emphasise the links and explore the relationships between ideas to demonstrate how things are connected
Review	Critically examine the topic Assess/appraise the main points Comment on observations
State	Clearly express the main points
Summarise	Briefly state the main points
Trace	Give an outline showing the development or history of the topic Describe the stages

Specific structures

Whilst at university, you will be expected to write in a variety of formats. Writing is a universal skill which gives you the opportunity to further explore your critical thinking skills (see Chapter 1).

How will I manage the amount of writing expected in my course?

What active learning strategies will you implement to provide you with a solid foundation for your writing skills?

As you will be required to interpret and respond to written assignments or exam instructions in your academic writing, you will need an active commitment to practise and refine your ability to think critically. Taking an Active Learning Approach to your writing in addition to using your critical thinking skills will provide you with a solid foundation for your writing. Whether you are writing an essay, report, summary, rationale or case study, these writing skills and your ability to think rationally and insightfully will enable you to acquire communication skills which are highly desirable in many careers.

> Read anything and everything.
> Be observant: look at the way an author begins sentences, connects ideas and links paragraphs.
> Look for structure in the writing.
> Make a list of connective words and interesting vocabulary which you can refer to in your own writing.
> Ask for and reflect on feedback.
> Practise writing for a range of purposes, using paragraph structures.

Each discipline area will have its own terminology which should be used in a way that demonstrates your understanding. Your topic details may provide specific instructions regarding style of writing, language, format and layout. Remember to follow this meticulously to ensure that you meet all the requirements.

Essay structure

The purpose of an essay is to demonstrate your understanding of a topic through research and investigation and then to develop a clear and reasoned response that is relevant to the key instructions in the essay topic.

Prior to beginning your essay you will need to establish its purpose and consider your audience. The following steps will assist you in this process.

Step 1: Identify the key instruction terms and understand the essay topic

Identify which parts of the essay topic are the instructions (action verbs). These will determine the style of writing your essay will require. For example, an essay that asks you to *explain* requires a different approach to one that asks you to *review* (see Table 2.5).

Make sure you understand all of the words contained in the topic and any terminology. Use a dictionary to look up any unfamiliar words. It is not possible to write a convincing essay that addresses the topic if you do not have a solid understanding of what you are being asked to do.

Determine the parameters of the topic. This will provide a reasonable focus and will limit the scope of your research.

Step 2: Research

Researching the topic will take time and will require you to read widely to find out what others have said on an issue, explore the relevant arguments raised, evaluate a position and draw conclusions.

Read more widely than the scope of the essay to increase your vocabulary and inform your understanding of the topic in general.

Step 3: Plan.

Take notes as you read and develop a plan (see Chapter 3). This research and planning stage will help you to gain a deeper understanding of an issue and enable you to begin to write.

An essay has three distinct parts: an introduction, a body and a conclusion.

Introduction

The first part of the essay, the introduction, will introduce the reader to the focus of the essay by establishing its purpose, stating the main contention and outlining the supporting arguments with regard to the question/topic. Your goal is to generate the reader's interest in the topic and encourage them to read on.

To heighten the reader's interest, you may also include:
> an interesting fact
> a surprising piece of information
> an exciting quotation
> a short narrative/anecdote
> a provocative question.

At this stage you do not include examples, figures or specific information. The relevant place for these is in the body of the essay.

Body of the essay

The body of the essay is where you explore the topic in detail using paragraphs to organise your ideas, remembering that each paragraph will have a clear, singular focus.

Within the body of the essay, you demonstrate your knowledge of the topic. Depending on the key instructions, you will examine different perspectives, anticipate and respond to counter arguments, include authoritative quotations, illustrate your main points with examples and support each point with valid evidence. This example indicates how a point of view may be substantiated using valid evidence:

> . . . *This approach reinforces the point of view held by Rowe (2010), that the more diversity in a system the more resilient it will be* . . .

Table 2.6 Refining individual paragraphs

Logic
Does your argument/sentence make sense?
How does it follow from what was said before?
Does it contradict a previous statement?
Is there one argument per paragraph?

Clarity
Could the argument or sentences have been expressed more clearly?
Have you selected the most appropriate word for the context?
Have you elaborated sufficiently in order for the meaning to be clear?
Is there any **ambiguity**?

Accuracy
Is the argument valid?
Has it been adequately supported with evidence?
Can you check the accuracy of the facts, statements and opinions?

Precision
Is there sufficient detail to explain what you mean?
How could you have been more specific?

Relevancy

Are your statements and ideas relevant to the question?

Do the sentences support the argument?

Depth

Have you adequately discussed and analysed the evidence in support of your argument?

Have you drawn conclusions from the evidence?

Conclusion

In this section you will recap the main ideas and summarise the essay. It is here that you move from the specific (which is included in the body) to the general; therefore, no new information is introduced. Your conclusion will confirm your initial statements in the introduction. In the conclusion, you will talk about the consequences or implications of the discussion, state what action needs to be taken, and reiterate and connect the main ideas. In addition, you may challenge the reader and be creative by including a thought-provoking quotation or statement or describing a powerful image in the final sentence. Remember that each aspect of your conclusion must relate to what you have said in the body of the essay and be relevant to the topic.

Does your conclusion draw the arguments together in support of the main contention? Have you summarised the key ideas? How have you qualified your position? Is there any new information which has not been previously mentioned? Do your final sentences connect to the question/topic?

Keep your conclusion short: don't include any new information!

Understanding the structure of an essay and the essay topic is only the beginning of the writing process. A good essay is the result of time, thought, careful planning and editing. The planning and writing stage is discussed in Chapter 3; however, essays have particular aspects of style which you will need to consider.

1. *Use the appropriate tense.* Essays may be written in the past or present tense. Always check your topic details to determine which tense is accepted in your discipline area.

2. *Select which voice to use.* Generally, essays are written in the third person ·'This essay will explore . . .'. However, in some cases the use of the first person is allowed in the introduction 'In this essay I will explore . . .'. Always check your topic details to determine which voice is accepted in your discipline area.
3. *Use quotations correctly.* Demonstrate your understanding of an issue by paraphrasing rather than using direct quotations where possible. Use direct quotations sparingly for greater impact.
4. *Use full, grammatically correct sentences.* In an academic essay, bullet points, lists and abbreviated sentences are rarely used.
5. An essay question generally does not have a correct answer.

Writing an essay is an opportunity to explore a topic, develop and elaborate a point of view, and draw conclusions that are supported by evidence. It is essential that whatever point of view you choose to promote, you support it with significant evidence and demonstrate a balanced and considered acknowledgement of the opposing views.

Report structure

At university, you may be required to write reports. All reports serve a similar purpose, which is to inform by presenting the facts of an issue and providing conclusions and recommendations for future action. A report may present research findings, survey results, an analysis of an issue, recommendations or a suggested plan of action.

Whatever format of report you use, consider who the report is for, the reader's level of knowledge on the topic and how the report will be used. This will determine what is contained in the report. Refer to your topic details for the parameters. Below is an example of a report topic outlining what is expected:

> *Prepare a report which identifies the sustainable initiatives implemented by your local council. Conduct a survey with relevant stakeholders to determine the effectiveness of these initiatives. Incorporate your findings and suggest recommendations for improvements.*

There are several different styles of report. Each style will have headings that guide you in selecting appropriate content for each section.

Introduction

The introduction includes the relevant background to the topic and the purpose; an explanation of why the report is being written and for whom; and the objectives. It also contains a statement to indicate the limitations and the scope of the report. The limitations refer to difficulties or obstacles that may have impacted on the results and recommendations of the report. Give a short, succinct **synopsis**. The number of words will be relative to the length of the report. Refer to your topic details.

Body

The body is the main part of the report and contains the methodology, discussion and analysis of the topic. The headings in the body of the report will vary depending on the style of the report. Generally, it can be assumed that the body will contain: method, procedure, results and discussion.

Method

This section outlines the way research was conducted – for example, materials, surveys, literature.

Procedure

This section lists the actions you took to collect the data/information (methodology) – that is, what you did and how you did it.

Results

This section incorporates the information you have collected.

This is where you state your findings – what happened. You may include relevant carefully selected tables, figures, charts and photos.

Discussion

This section examines the results and discusses the reasons for the results. It might also discuss any discrepancies which may have impacted on the results, or surprising findings. The analysis of your findings will confirm the adequacy of the methodology.

Within this section you can explore the application of theory to support the **premise** of your report.

This information should be presented in a logical sequence using headings and sub-headings. Headings are used to introduce a new idea or sections, and sub-headings narrow the perspective. Under the headings and sub-headings, paragraphs will contain one idea and show clear connections.

Conclusion

The conclusion is a summary of the main points and the findings from within the body of the report. There must be a clear connection between the content of the introduction and the conclusion.

Consider the following questions as you develop your conclusion:

> Have you achieved the report's objectives (purpose)?
> Was the methodology appropriate?
> Have you covered everything you said you would cover?
> Have you covered it in enough detail?

Recommendations

The recommendations will be based on your findings in the conclusion. You will use critical thinking skills to question those findings and then determine whether any issues or problems were identified by the results. This, together with the analysis in the discussion section, will enable you to develop a list of realistic recommendations. These recommendations may incorporate suggestions for future improvements or actions, to promote further discussion, or to propose further investigation. Your recommendations must include a realistic statement that clearly defines how the recommendations might be implemented: this may include feasibility statements, priorities and time considerations.

References

This section lists all the sources you have used within the report, appropriately referenced.

Glossary

The glossary includes terminology, topic-specific vocabulary, acronyms and abbreviations referred to in the report, including a supporting definition.

Appendices

This section contains attachments which are too large to include in the body of the report. It is additional information for the reader, but it can only be included when it has been directly referred to in the text. An appendix may include maps, questionnaires, legislation, tables, data, graphs, specifications and pictures.

Report writing aspects of style

- Develop clear, precise and grammatically correct sentences.
- Be clear and unambiguous.
- State relevant information in bullet point form (where appropriate).
- Include appropriate terminology.
- Clarify information with tables, figures and maps.
- Use the third person; however, check your topic details and school house style guide.
- Select the passive or active voice according to the topic details.
- Incorporate inclusive language.

Case study structure

A case study is another distinctive form of academic writing. It is an in-depth study of a particular person, group or event and describes issues, problems and challenges that need to be investigated. In a case study you examine a particular aspect of a real-life situation and apply your knowledge of the theories to the context.

There are two common approaches used in case studies. The first is to use an analytical approach, where a situation is examined to facilitate an understanding of what is happening and to explore the reasons why.

The second method involves a problem-oriented approach, where an issue is investigated from theoretical and practical perspectives to identify problems and make recommendations.

Either approach will require you to explore and gather data, to think critically and to employ your active learning skills to analyse a real-life situation. This process is an exciting opportunity that enables you to use your higher-order analytical and synthesis thinking skills.

The following are general guidelines for structure, which may vary depending on the approach used, the parameters of the case study and your topic details. In this example of case study structure, the broad headings have been numbered for clarification.

1. Case background

This section of the case study provides contextual information needed to understand the particular case. It presents the relevant background and key points in a summarised format.

2. Body of the report

The body of a case study report contains two headings. These assist you to organise the information you have gathered into a logical and sequential order. The heading titles in the body of the case study will differ according to the case study's purpose and style.

a. *A statement of the case issues* (focuses on *What?* questions. What caused this?)
  > Identify and state the major problems or issues in priority order. (Your case study may reveal problems that are occurring, or you may identify potential issues that may cause problems in the future.)
  > Differentiate between long-term and short-term issues or problems and prioritise.
  > Link the issues and problems to the relevant theories.

b. *A statement of the key problems and issues* (focuses on *Why?* questions. Why are they problems?)
  > Explore the symptoms of the issues or problems. (These should refer to your statement in the previous section.)
  > Analyse the problems in relation to theory.
  > Examine the impact of the problems.
  > Develop a hypothesis as to why the problems may have occurred.
  > Draw conclusions and support your conclusions with evidence (from the case study, research and the relevant theory).

3. Alternative solutions (focuses on *What if?* questions. What are the options?)

> Consider all options.
> Identify potential solutions to the problems.
> Examine potential *methods* for resolving the problems.
> Develop criteria for evaluating potential solutions.
> Explore the impact of the proposed solutions.
> Evaluate the advantages and disadvantages against your evaluation criteria.

4. Recommendations (addresses *Who?*, *What?*, *When?* and *How?* questions)

> Prioritise your recommendations based on the problems identified in the previous sections.
> Provide a rationale for adopting the recommendations.
> Develop a detailed implementation (action) plan with contingencies.
> Identify the **pragmatic** details: Who will be responsible? What needs to happen? When does it need to happen? How will success be measured?
> Provide current, sufficient, reliable and authentic evidence to support your implementation.
> Justify the recommendations through the application of theory to the implementation plan. (Why is this the best approach?)

5. References

A list of all the materials you have used within the case study, appropriately referenced.

6. Appendices

Appendices are attachments to the main document which are too large to include in the body of the case study. It is additional information for the reader, but can only be included when it has been directly referred to in the text. Appendices may include relevant background, research material, organisational information, policies, procedures, forms and pictures.

A case study is more than a description of a situation. It requires you to research in depth, gather data, analyse and synthesise information, and demonstrate your knowledge and understanding of the relevant theory. The outcome of a case study is the identification of a pragmatic resolution to an issue, which is supported by a comprehensive analysis of the situation and a list of pertinent recommendations.

Academic writing style summary

Understanding the structures of an essay, report and case study is only the beginning of the writing process. Constructing a good essay, report or case study is the result of time, thought, careful planning and editing. Learning how to plan, craft your words and create effective pieces of writing is discussed in Chapter 3.

Regardless of the type of academic writing you use, always check your school house style guide and topic details for instructions relating to the presentation format. The guide will list the size of font, the spacing between sentences and lines, the hierarchy of headings, the reference style, and the page number format, along with many other specific features.

Study aids

The College's website includes a number of interactive study aids (such as clinical communication, basic drug calculations, basic life support, mental health) which may assist you in your studies and practice: http://www.flinders.edu.au/nursing/studentsandcourses/resources-for-students/resources-for-students.cfm#.

Professional Language Development

English language and communication classes, online activities, and other resources are offered at no cost for College of Nursing and Health Sciences students. The program varies and is nursing/midwifery specific.

Find the timetable on Professional Language Development in your FLO topic list: https://flo.flinders.edu.au/course/view.php?id=4234.

Student Learning Centre

The Student Learning Centre at Flinders offers a variety of help for students, including a Writing Centre, a Maths Centre, drop-ins and individual consultations, study skills, grammar and numeracy leaflets, online learning materials, and academic skills programs. Opening hours, program, service and study guide information is available here: www.flinders.edu.au/current-students/slc/.

Chapter summary

Each form of academic writing has a purpose and a series of unique features. These are summarised in Table 2.7.

Table 2.7 Academic writing comparative table

	Essay	Report	Case study
Purpose	To demonstrate your understanding of a topic through research and investigation, and then to develop a clear and reasoned response	To inform and present the facts of an issue, with conclusions and recommendations for future action	To investigate and analyse a real life situation in depth, which may incorporate problem identification and potential solutions
Structure	Written using well-developed paragraphs Introduction Body of evidence Conclusion	Introduction Body (Method Procedure Results Discussion) Conclusion Recommendations References Glossary Appendix/ices	Case background Body (statement of case issues, causes of problems) Alternative solutions Recommendations Reference Appendix/ices
Style	Formal Presents a balanced view and therefore may have some subjective elements Uses evidence to illustrate and support ideas and concepts	Formal and objective Uses theory to illustrate Incorporates relevant graphics and tables to illustrate and explain	Formal, informative Applies theory to practice Includes relevant graphics and tables in an appendix
Format	Usually no headings or sub-headings Check your topic details, as some disciplines allow prescribed headings	Uses headings and sub-headings to organise the information Bullet points may be used	Uses headings and sub-headings to organise the information

Writing in the academic environment will require time and commitment. This style of writing will reinforce your knowledge and understanding of theory, refine your critical thinking and reading skills, and enlarge your vocabulary.

Effective academic writing demonstrates your understanding and synthesis of the theory you are learning by containing:

》 a logical sequence
》 a valid premise
》 supporting evidence
》 a rational argument.

Your ability to demonstrate these writing skills will ensure your success in the academic environment and will be highly valued in the workplace and the community.

Summary activities

1. List the three main styles of writing used in the academic environment and identify the different formats.
2. What is the purpose of writing a report in comparison to an essay?
3. When would you use a case study in preference to a report?
4. How does a report differ in structure from an essay?
5. Why do we use paragraphs to structure a piece of writing?
6. What are the purposes of the parts of a paragraph?
7. Describe the grammatical features you will use to add formality to your writing.
8. How will you approach an essay that requires you to 'examine' an issue, in contrast to one that requires you to 'argue'?
9. How does the consideration of audience and purpose impact your style of writing?
10. Write a sentence that illustrates the use of active voice. Rewrite the sentence in the passive voice.

Reflection

》 Which areas of academic writing challenge you?
》 Why do these aspects challenge you?
》 How will you overcome them?

Photo credit

67 © Photoroller/Shutterstock.

3 Express Yourself!
Create effective writing

Learning Outcomes

By the end of this chapter you will have strategies which enable you to:

> plan, draft, write and review a piece of writing
> enrich your vocabulary
> present a piece of writing that is clear and legible
> structure a piece of academic writing
> link your ideas in a sequential and cohesive manner
> use grammar and punctuation for meaning
> select a style of writing for a particular purpose – report, essay or case study
> follow the conventions for academic writing.

Your objective when writing in an academic style is to present a well-structured piece of writing that states a position, develops an argument or builds a case, and uses facts and evidence to support this position. To create a piece of writing that effectively meets this objective requires a conscientious and diligent approach to planning, researching, drafting and editing. As you read widely and become familiar with your subject area, you will increase your knowledge of the specific vocabulary, technical terms, theories, concepts and academic ideas. This, together with feedback from your lecturers and tutors, will enable you to become confident and capable in formulating and expressing your own ideas and theories using your own words. Through this process, your writing skills will develop and improve as you find your distinct style of writing.

From the outset, using your active learning skills will empower you to approach the task of writing with a purpose. This begins with exploring ideas, defining research parameters, locating relevant information, organising findings, thinking critically and developing an informed point of view. Each of these steps informs the development of a writing plan, which will enable you to structure your ideas and guide you in the drafting and editing phases.

Strategies to get you going!

Time management – planning your assignment program

An essential part of a successful writing process involves the skills of sound planning, time management and prioritising. A realistic work schedule will allow you to complete and hand in your work by the due date. This will involve allocating time to each stage of the writing process, including analysis, research, planning, drafting, editing, referencing and proofreading.

Figure 3.1 outlines a suggested timeframe for writing a 2000 word essay.

Week one		Week two		Week three		Week four	
Analyse your topic and brain-storm	Begin your research	Construct a detailed plan	Write your first draft	Edit and redraft	Finalise your reference list	Proof-read your work	Submit your work on time!

Figure 3.1 Assignment time management plan

Remember that wise planning from the start equips you to manage your time efficiently and limit your stress, and enables you to produce a well-researched, carefully considered and crafted piece of writing.

Strategies for taking notes

At university, students are required to develop a range of skills to support their learning: some of which may be new. Active listening, effective reading and note taking are three such skills, and frequently students do not realise their importance. Information presented in lectures and tutorials often contains the central concepts of the course and the material most likely to be included in exams. Additionally, much of your time will be spent in collating and recording research from a variety of sources. As an active learner, it is essential that you quickly learn to take effective notes to support your learning at university.

Taking accurate, relevant notes is crucial to successful writing and is relevant to all academic learning environments: lectures, tutorials, teamwork, independent study and FLO. The main purpose of note taking is to record your understanding of the ideas and concepts discussed in lectures and tutorials and to make use of these notes in your writing. (Note taking is also essential for revision and exam preparation.)

Recording accurate notes allows you to:

- recall what you have read or heard
- record relevant information
- identify the main points and key ideas
- explore theories
- synthesise new information
- formulate your own view
- express new information in your own words
- maintain a record of references
- develop a permanent record for revision.

Developing effective note taking requires an Active Learning Approach: listening for a purpose, identifying cues given by the lecturer, employing effective reading strategies (see Chapter 6), and expressing these in your own words wherever possible. There are a wide variety of note-taking techniques; however, creating your own system for recording ideas, concepts and theories in your own words greatly enhances your understanding. You may find that you employ a variety of methods and ways of organising ideas depending on your purpose for note taking. Regardless of the technique you adopt, it is imperative that you record the author, date, title, publisher and other referencing details for each source, including lectures, workshops, written and audio material, to avoid plagiarism.

Avoiding plagiarism

Plagiarism involves using the words, thoughts, ideas and images of others without acknowledgement and is regarded as fraud. However, there are techniques for legally incorporating the ideas of others in your own writing: directly quoting, summarising and paraphrasing with references are recognised strategies for acknowledging others and avoiding plagiarism (see Chapter 4).

It is absolutely essential that you acknowledge each and every source used, regardless of whether you have rephrased the ideas in your own words. Always remember that ideas, thoughts, concepts and theories remain the work of the original author.

Establishing a technique which best suits your preferred learning style will assist you in becoming a proficient note taker. A commonly used technique is the linear method of note taking.

Linear note-taking method

A linear note-taking method is a preferred method for taking notes as it allows you to record information sequentially. Your notes follow the order of the points made, which makes it easier to revise and recall. When you use this method, whether in lectures or when taking notes from reading material, the following strategies may be useful:

> Set up a double page in your notebook or a table in a word processing document: on the right side record notes and annotate the left side (see Figure 3.2).
> Use coloured pens/fonts to differentiate between your own thoughts and the ideas of others, to show connections, to emphasise a point and to determine areas to research.
> Underline key words.
> Surround important points in a box, or use an asterisk or bold type.
> Insert quotation marks to indicate a quotation (to distinguish between your own words and another author's words).

> Summarise and paraphrase new information. (If you are using electronic sources of information, ensure you use your own words rather than copy and paste sections of text.)

> Use symbols and abbreviations when note taking (see Figure 3.3).

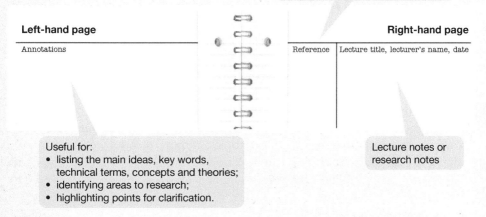

Referencing details (including page numbers)
NB These may be sources referred to by the lecturer

Left-hand page

Annotations

Right-hand page

| Reference | Lecture title, lecturer's name, date |

Useful for:
• listing the main ideas, key words, technical terms, concepts and theories;
• identifying areas to research;
• highlighting points for clarification.

Lecture notes or research notes

Figure 3.2 Linear note taking

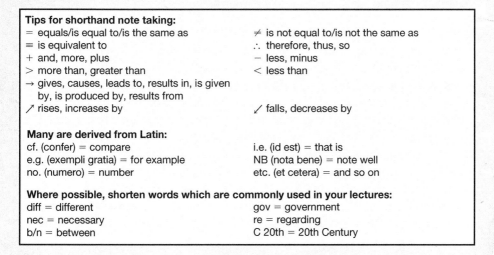

Tips for shorthand note taking:

$=$ equals/is equal to/is the same as	$\neq$ is not equal to/is not the same as
$\equiv$ is equivalent to	$\therefore$ therefore, thus, so
$+$ and, more, plus	$-$ less, minus
$>$ more than, greater than	$<$ less than
$\rightarrow$ gives, causes, leads to, results in, is given by, is produced by, results from	
$\nearrow$ rises, increases by	$\searrow$ falls, decreases by

Many are derived from Latin:

cf. (confer) = compare	i.e. (id est) = that is
e.g. (exempli gratia) = for example	NB (nota bene) = note well
no. (numero) = number	etc. (et cetera) = and so on

Where possible, shorten words which are commonly used in your lectures:

diff = different	gov = government
nec = necessary	re = regarding
b/n = between	C 20th = 20th Century

Figure 3.3 Suggested symbols and abbreviations for note taking

Taking comprehensive notes enables you to develop a deeper understanding of a topic. However, in order to analyse and **assimilate** the information and apply it to a writing task, you will need to explore the ideas, look at the parts and establish the connections. A brainstorm approach or constructing a concept map are creative and flexible strategies for doing this. These methods provide a visual representation of your thoughts and ideas around the topic.

Brainstorming

Using a brainstorming technique for exploring ideas allows you to expand your thinking or plan your response. It gives you the opportunity to investigate any and every idea before refining and organising your thinking in a more structured way.

When using the brainstorming method, you begin by writing your topic or area of study in the centre of a blank page. You then work outwards, linking new ideas and thoughts as you think of them, whilst building a picture of your topic. In this process you may be as creative as you like! You can use colours, pictures, words and symbols to record any ideas, topics, authors, theories, or anything else related to your topic. Your ideas can be placed anywhere on the page and you can make associations and links as freely as you like. At this point, you do not need to filter anything out; as you research further, you will sift through the ideas which are of most relevance and ignore the rest. (See Figure 3.4.)

Concept maps

Concept maps are often used to graphically illustrate the relationships between concepts or the main ideas of a topic. The rationale which underpins concept maps stems from the **Constructivist Theory** (developed as an assimilation of the work of a number of theorists, including Piaget, Dewey, Vygotsky and Bruner), where new information and ideas are acquired and incorporated into the framework of existing knowledge in order to construct meaning. In constructing a concept map, you build a framework based on what you already know about a topic, integrate new knowledge into that structure, and identify and confirm connections. Your learning becomes more meaningful as you internalise and act on new understandings which will effectively inform your writing plan.

Concept maps are generally regarded as a creative and innovative method for formulating your thoughts around a specific topic. Concept maps assist you to:

> focus your research
> identify challenges

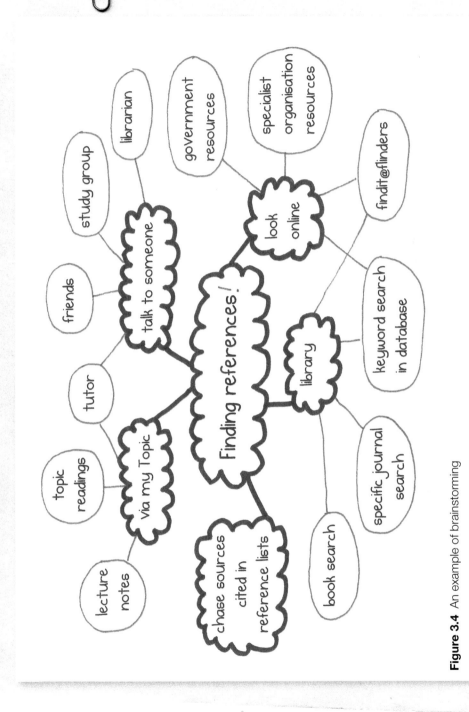

Figure 3.4 An example of brainstorming

- organise your ideas
- discover relationships between ideas and concepts
- enhance and encourage your understanding
- develop a structure for an assignment.

In a concept map, two or more concepts are linked by words that describe their relationship. To construct a map, you begin with your topic written in the middle of the page and arrange the main ideas and key points around it. You then map the relationships between the ideas or key points using lines, arrows, colours and words to link them to the main topic and/or each other. In this process you are more able to identify the type of relationship or link between the points – for instance, cause and effect, similarity, contrast, consequence, parallelism.

Figure 3.5 is a sample concept map which refers to the following essay topic:

> Describe all the factors you need to consider when caring for a patient with asthma.

By arranging your ideas and concepts showing the connections, you create the structure for your assignment and this will inform the stages of your writing: research, planning, drafting and editing.

> For note-taking purposes, consider that in lectures concept maps may be more difficult to use when recording the key words and ideas, as you do not have all the information in front of you. However, this does not mean that you cannot use a concept map to enhance your understanding and record what you have just heard a lecturer explain, and then add to it as you learn and research further.

The writing process

The writing process begins with analysing the topic or question, defining research parameters, locating relevant information, organising findings, thinking critically and developing an informed point of view. These steps inform the development of a writing plan, which will enable you to structure your ideas and guide you through the drafting, editing and proofreading phases (see Figure 3.6).

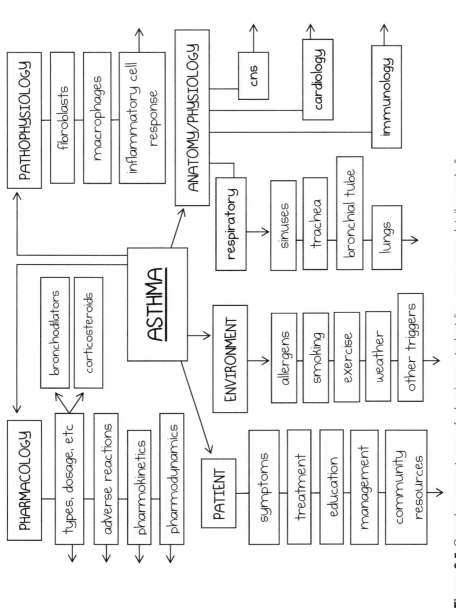

Figure 3.5 Sample concept map of a beginner student (i.e. many more details needed)

| Analyse | Research | Plan | Draft | Edit | Proofread |

Figure 3.6 Steps in the writing process

1. Analyse the question/topic

When preparing to produce a piece of academic writing, irrespective of what format it may take, it is essential that you have a sound understanding of your topic. This ensures that you correctly interpret and address every aspect of the assignment question/topic and produce a structured and accurate written response. The key to this and the first step in any academic writing process is to correctly analyse the question/topic.

Interpret the assignment question/topic and identify the key instruction terms

Understanding your topic is an integral part of the writing process. You will need to:
> identify instruction words
> recognise content/key words and phrases
> determine limiting words and phrases
> confirm your current knowledge in relation to the topic
> associate relevant theories to the topic.

Identify instruction words

First, dissect the topic and identify which parts are the instruction words: such as *compare*, *define*, *investigate*, *explore*. Ensure that you understand the meaning of these directions and you are clear on what is required; these will inform how you structure your writing. Refer to Chapter 2, Table 2.5. If there are any unfamiliar words or terminology you do not understand, use a dictionary or other resource to find out.

Instruction word

Australia needs a sustainable healthcare strategy. <u>Debate</u> the impact of this.

Recognise content/key words and phrases

In order to define the topic area, you will need to recognise the content or key words and phrases. These will establish the general focus of the topic and guide your analysis.

  Key word   *Key phrase*   *Key word*

<u>Australia</u> needs a <u>sustainable healthcare strategy</u>. <u>Debate</u> the <u>impact</u> of this.

Determine limiting words and phrases

Determine the parameters of the topic by identifying words or phrase which indicate the scope of the topic. For example:

Compare <u>two scenarios</u> . . .

Determine the <u>major</u> problems in the system . . .

. . . in the light of <u>current</u> social changes . . .

. . . consider the impact of this <u>on Australia</u> . . .

This will provide you with a reasonable focus, which will limit the scope of your research and overall, make the topic more manageable.

Confirm your current knowledge and associate relevant theory to the topic

Next, you will need to relate the topic to what you currently know and identify relevant theories. This will provide you with direction for your research and assist in your planning.

You may find it helpful to write the topic down on a blank piece of paper and use the brainstorming process to enhance your interpretation of the topic and allow you to more easily make connections between your thoughts and ideas.

Brainstorming and concept maps

Brainstorming can be an effective way to produce ideas on a specific assignment topic. Using the brainstorm method, you freely explore the topic and generate ideas, concepts and opinions which radiate from the central theme. This enables you to determine the connections between ideas and identify a plan of action.

Once you have read and understood the topic, you draw on your general knowledge about the topic, together with your lecture and tutorial notes, to begin brainstorming. This process is not limiting in any way and allows you to explore everything that comes to mind. As you work through this creative process you will more clearly identify the ideas you wish to pursue, and you will develop an awareness of the concepts and ideas which require further research.

In your deliberations/brainstorm, you might consider:

> words you need to define
> ideas triggered by the topic
> links to related theories
> concepts and ideas to research
> information from your own general knowledge which might be used to support a point of view or
> points or questions you may need to clarify.

See Figures 3.4 and 3.5 as examples.

You may find that when you look at a topic, no ideas come to mind. Think laterally. Do not panic! Instead, walk away from it for a few hours, or review your notes and readings, before coming back to consider the topic from a different perspective. Talk to a friend. You may find that once you get started, brainstorming will stimulate your thinking and random thoughts will begin to flow. As you note these down you will discover connections, your thoughts will become more organised and logical, areas for research will become evident and your perspective will become clearer. From here you can develop a more organised plan of action to inform the next steps in the writing process.

Consider the amount of paper you use. Use both sides of the page in a notebook, in preference to single pieces of paper that can be lost.

2. Research

This is an exciting part of the writing process, where you have the opportunity to explore a sample of the vast body of knowledge on a particular topic. Research informs and enlightens you; it broadens your understanding and reveals perspectives you may not otherwise have considered.

Research is more than gathering and remembering facts: it involves looking at the facts from different perspectives, drawing connections between concepts and theories, and integrating them into your own body of work. Benjamin Bloom (1956), an educational academic, developed a mastery learning theory which classified lower and higher **cognitive** thinking levels. His theory can be applied to inform an effective research approach where research begins with acquiring knowledge and ends with the evaluation and synthesis of that information. Therefore, when you research:

> read and understand (interpret, paraphrase, summarise)
> analyse (appraise, compare, contrast, organise)
> evaluate (question, justify, make judgements, assess, draw conclusions)
> synthesise (hypothesise, formulate, compose) the information.

Begin your research

Once you have understood the assignment question/topic and determined your immediate direction, you are ready to identify the external parameters of the task. These will be listed in your topic details and may include:

> the number and type of research materials you are required to reference
> any specific sources you are required to access
> the parameters which may determine the currency of your research (for example, 'Reference must be made to research conducted post-2000.').

However, whilst you may be given a prescriptive number and type of research material, aim to read more widely to broaden your understanding. Reading and assimilating information from a range of resources will inform and enrich your writing.

> Use the resources that are immediately available to you to do a quick reconnaissance of the words, phrases or technical terms that you identified as a result of your brainstorm. A dictionary and thesaurus are valuable tools at this stage to enhance your understanding of the key words, along with an encyclopaedia, the internet and library catalogues. This enables you to develop your ideas further and to formulate new ones. Do not spend too long in this stage – it is just an overview to stimulate your ideas further.

> Identify potential sources of information. These may include:
  - lecture and tutorial notes
  - topic reading list
  - subject guides held in the university library
  - journal articles (the library holds a list of journals relevant to your topic discipline)
  - books
  - institutional websites
  - experts in the field (for example, lecturers, academic staff).

Locate the resources

Your next step is to locate sources of information; however, it is vital that you are clear about the parameters of your research and that you understand the assignment question using the strategies identified in step 1 of the writing process.

Develop a list of the key words related to your search topic. Use your assigned pre-reading, lecture notes and brainstorming ideas to identify those words that are relevant to the topic. Make a list of synonyms of these key words. (Using a thesaurus is a good strategy for this.)

Asthma treatments

A list of related words and/or synonyms may include:

adult, childhood, inhalers, preventers, nebulisers, spacers, environmental triggers, side effects.

This list of key words will keep you focused on the topic and guide your research using relevant databases and other sources of information.

Access the library and select the most relevant database. If you are unsure about how to do this, talk to your Liaison Librarian. Librarians have a wealth of knowledge and experience in research and are an invaluable resource.

Access the database using your key words with the appropriate:

- **Boolean operators** (and/or/not) or search for an exact phrase
- quotation marks "air pollution"
- **truncation** function, which allows you to substitute an * for one or more letters within a word; this is particularly useful, as the database will search for variations of the key word. (For example, renew* may **elicit** renewable, renewing, renewed, renews.)

At this point in the research process your search may reveal a very large number of resources. Use these strategies to reduce the number of results:

> Re-evaluate your key words – are they too broad?
> Construct a new search phrase using additional key words.
> Narrow the search by using quotation marks to specify groups of words that belong together as a single phrase.
> Check the spelling and construction of your search words/phrase.
> Use the database search tools to limit the search to the journal title or the journal abstract.
> Seek assistance from a librarian.

Begin your research with general texts to gain an overview; then progress to other sources.

A search of the library database and the internet will reveal a range of sources, including (but not limited to) e-journals, print-based journals, government publications, books and conference papers. Your next step is to determine the relevance and authenticity of the information. Use the following as a guide:

Authentic:
Is the information from a reliable source?
Has it been written by someone of authority in the field?
Who is the publisher?
What is the origin of the source?

Relevant:
Are the keywords located in the abstract of the journal?
Does the table of contents contain the key words or main themes?
Do the chapters have relevant sub-headings?
Is the content related to the topic?

Current:
How up to date is the information?
How does this impact on your research?
Have you considered the original sources of ideas, concepts and theories?

There are instances where it is absolutely necessary to read, understand and refer to work regardless of the publication date, as past research informs more recent bodies of work.

Audience and purpose:
For whom is the information intended?
Why was it written?

These questions will assist you to pass an initial judgement about the validity of a source prior to reading it in depth. The list of resources you now have available to you forms the starting point of your reading. You will return again and again to the research phase as you read and then begin your writing drafts. This initial phase of research should elicit enough reading for you to gain a broad understanding of the topic, to ignite your ideas, to ask questions, and to begin formulating a premise for your writing.

Checklist for evaluating Web sources

Use these criteria for evaluating websites:

1. **Source.** What organisation sponsors the website? Look for the site's owner at the top or bottom of the home page or in the Web address. Enter the owner's name on Google or another search engine to learn about the organisation. If a website doesn't indicate ownership, you have to make a judgment about who put it up and why.

2. **Author.** Is the author identified? (Look for an 'About Us' link if you see no author listed.) Enter the name in a search engine to learn more about the author. Websites often give no information about their authors other than an email address or Twitter handle, and sometimes not even that. That makes it difficult or impossible to determine the author's qualifications. Be cautious about information on anonymous sites.

3. **Purpose.** Is the website trying to sell you something? Many websites are infomercials that might contain useful information, but they are no more trustworthy than other forms of advertising. Is the purpose to entertain? To inform? To persuade?

4. **Timeliness.** When was the website last updated? Look for a date on the home page. Many Web pages do not list when they were last updated; thus you cannot determine their currency.

5. **Evidence.** Are sources of information listed? Factual information should be supported by indicating where the information came from—reliable websites will list and link to their sources.

6. **Biases.** Does the website offer a balanced point of view? Many websites conceal their attitude with a reasonable tone and seemingly factual evidence such as statistics. Citations and bibliographies do not ensure that a site is reliable. Look carefully at the links and sources cited, and peruse the 'About Us' link if one is available.

7. **Intended audience.** What audience is the website targeting? Is this a website aimed at healthcare consumers or healthcare professionals? If you are writing a paper as a healthcare professional student, the use of websites aimed at healthcare consumers is unlikely to provide the depth of information and appropriate levels of evidence required to adequately inform your knowledge.

Organise the research

It is vital that you develop a system to manage your resource material and that you make a firm commitment to maintain your management system. You might consider the following:

> Set up folders on your computer/USB.
> Use manila folders or dividers/pockets for hard copies.
> Annotate every article, paper, photocopy with the referencing details, including page numbers.

Having sourced, organised and referenced the initial research material you need, it is time to begin reading and taking effective notes.

Reduce what you need to print. Save articles onto your USB or home drive.

Evaluate the research

The next phase of the planning process involves making informed decisions about which articles are most relevant to the point of view you are developing. Consider the articles you have collected, together with your annotated notes, and sift through the ideas looking for common themes. It may be helpful to colour code the articles, or mark and collate them, to classify them according to the themes in your argument.

Identify the key articles/resources that are pivotal to your main point, focusing on the requirements for the number and types of sources you are permitted to refer to in your written piece. Reassess each of the selected articles and ask yourself:

> Is this article relevant to the topic?
> What is the author's main point?
> Have I understood the main point?
> What evidence does the author use to support the point of view?

This process will assist you to develop your premise which will underpin your writing. A **premise** is the position around which you construct your writing; it is supported with evidence and is the basis for drawing conclusions. It will also assist you to establish the main arguments, which are a series of statements to persuade the reader.

Applying a variation of the Strengths, Weaknesses, Opportunities and Threats (SWOT) analysis may assist you to clarify and reduce the number of resources to only those which are pertinent (see Figure 3.7). As you assess each resource using this strategy, continually refer back to your topic to maintain your focus.

In evaluating the resources, you will confirm, consolidate and refine your ideas. At this point of the research phase, stop researching and take the time to critically think about what you have read. Review your notes and reconstruct your original

Strengths	Weaknesses
Are the author's main points valid?	Are there any inconsistencies, ambiguities or unsupported claims in the author's argument?
How do they relate to the premise?	
How do they enhance the arguments which support your premise?	What are the implications of using the argument in your own writing?

Opportunities	Threats
How can you use the author's argument to support your own premise?	Will the author's argument support or undermine your premise?
Does this provide an alternative way of considering the question/topic?	Is the source authentic, reliable and authoritative? If not, will it discredit your writing?

Figure 3.7 SWOT analysis

brainstorm or formulate a new one. This can be a useful strategy to organise your thoughts, consolidate the links between ideas, identify the key arguments which will support your premise, and formulate a sound position from which to state your case. Ensure that you have adequate evidence from your research to support your arguments and draw reasonable conclusions.

3. Develop a writing plan

Before you begin to write, it is essential that you are clear about the premise you are going to adopt in your writing. This may be a statement of fact, an argument or an opinion. Irrespective, it is vital that you are able to support your premise and validate it with evidence, as it will direct your writing from the outset.

If you are still unclear about your premise, revisit the topic; check your brainstorm, re-evaluate your notes and check the SWOT analysis to determine a possible direction. Frequently, an author's point of view may challenge you; however, thinking laterally may stimulate your ideas and enable you to formulate your own premise.

The next step prior to writing is to establish the audience for, and purpose of, your writing. Clearly, an assignment is intended for a particular topic lecturer and tutor; however, it is still valid to take into account who will read your piece of writing. Next, establish the purpose. Once you have determined your premise and the arguments that will support it, take the time to determine how you will structure your writing.

Use the key ideas and related themes (identified in your final brainstorm) to clarify the arguments that support your premise and collate the corresponding evidence for each one. Evaluating each of the arguments, and considering the most effective method of presenting them, will help you to establish a logical framework for your writing. Balancing two opposing views, demonstrating a cause-and-effect relationship or setting out a chronological progression of ideas, are three possible methods. Figure 3.8 is a linear method for organising your notes and formulating a detailed writing framework. It is a visual representation which enables you to confirm the connection between the main contention and the supporting arguments, to prioritise and sequence the ideas, and to determine the appropriate evidence. Use this diagram (Figure 3.8) to develop your writing plan.

4. Write a first draft

It is important when you begin to write your draft that you *just write*. This is known as 'free writing' and was formalised by Peter Elbow (1998), who stated: 'The goal of free writing is in the process not the product.' The focus at this initial stage is to get your ideas down and develop a logical argument using your plan as the guideline. Initially, it is more important that you express your thoughts, integrate the research and incorporate the work of others, without deliberating over accurate phrasing and the use of complex language; this will be considered in more detail in the editing phase.

Prepare your writing space

Prepare as follows:
> Locate a place where you feel motivated to write without distractions.
> Set up your workspace: consider adequate lighting, ergonomic implications, the space required and schedule regular breaks.
> Place the question/topic prominently and arrange your notes, relevant books, articles and online resources close by.
> Establish goals for your writing.

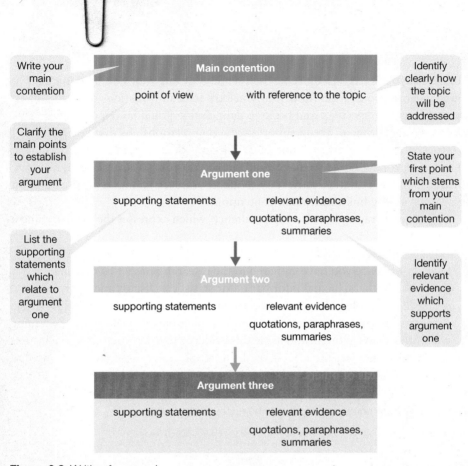

Write your main contention

Clarify the main points to establish your argument

List the supporting statements which relate to argument one

Main contention

point of view   with reference to the topic

Identify clearly how the topic will be addressed

Argument one

supporting statements   relevant evidence

quotations, paraphrases, summaries

State your first point which stems from your main contention

Argument two

supporting statements   relevant evidence

quotations, paraphrases, summaries

Identify relevant evidence which supports argument one

Argument three

supporting statements   relevant evidence

quotations, paraphrases, summaries

Figure 3.8 Writing framework

Create notepads using recycled paper.

Quality writing is the result of drafting and editing. It is unlikely that you will complete your writing task in one sitting; therefore, set realistic and achievable targets. The amount of time you spend writing on any one occasion will depend upon a number of factors, including your physical comfort, mental fatigue, personal efficiency and other commitments. It is important that you establish a healthy balance.

Begin writing

Initially, let your ideas flow and construct sentences using your writing framework as a guide. Through the process of writing you look at the information you have collated from different perspectives and begin to gain clarity: potential opportunities may emerge for exploring an argument or discovering relationships that you had not previously considered. At the same time, you may identify flaws in your argument. In this case, you will need to make a judgement: do you discard the idea, research it further, or think of an effective way to incorporate it? You must ensure that you maintain a strong link to the main contention.

Begin each paragraph with a topic sentence, which expresses the main argument to be discussed.

> Develop a series of sentences which elaborate this argument and present the relevant evidence you have gathered in the research phase; this may include the ideas of others, factual information or statistics. Discuss and analyse the evidence to establish the connection to the argument. This may be achieved by comparing or contrasting points of view, commenting on, qualifying or critiquing what others have written, and using this evidence to draw your own conclusions and construct a case. Table 3.1 provides a sample of phrases that may be used to present the ideas of others.

Table 3.1 Sample phrases (using the author–date reference style)

reveals	Research conducted by Rice (2009) reveals . . .
claims	In contrast, Gould (2010) claims . . .
suggests	Kelly and Templeman (2006) suggest . . .
consider	Kelly et al. (2006) consider an alternative approach in their research . . .
proposes	Gould (2010) proposes . . .
opposing view	An opposing view is presented by Templeman (2009).
notes	The implications of this approach are explored by Megarrell (2010), who notes . . .
argues	Rice (2007) argues . . .

> Carefully select the evidence you include, ensuring it is relevant and contributes to the point you are making, and diligently acknowledge and reference all sources of information.

> Write with clarity, expressing and elaborating on the ideas to make connections between the evidence and your argument.
> Use key words to keep the reader focused.
> Develop a progression of ideas using connective words (see Activity 3.1).

Rice (2007) proposes . . . . However, Gould (2010) suggests . . .
The implications of this approach are explored by Kelly et al. (2006, p. 5) who note . . . . In contrast, Megarrell (2010) argues . . .

> In your discussion you may draw attention to the limitations, generalisations or assumptions contained in the evidence which might give credence to your argument.

Kelly and Templeman (2010, p. 49) suggest . . . . Nevertheless, the results are based on a very small sample . . . .

> Use words to illustrate a relationship between ideas or to emphasise a point.

Without question, the research conducted by Rice (2009, p. 12) reveals that . . .
Above all, the implications of this approach are . . .

> The length of your paragraphs will differ according to the complexity of the idea you are examining and the evidence you use to elaborate the point. Your writing framework will assist you to identify the appropriate length and relevant content.
> Conclude each paragraph with a statement that links to the argument and **segues** smoothly into the next argument.

As you write, continually refer to your writing framework and the topic or question to develop and establish a robust argument. At the conclusion of writing your initial draft, read through it and note the flow of ideas, the links between each argument and the connections to the main contention. Consider whether further evidence is required to support or expand an idea; reorganise your sentences if necessary. With your initial ideas down, you now have a working document and you can begin to construct paragraphs to develop your ideas further.

The last step in the initial draft is to write the introductory and concluding paragraphs.

> The introductory paragraph establishes the purpose, states the main contention and outlines the supporting arguments with regard to the question/topic. This provides the reader with an overview of the position you have adopted, the perspective taken, and a definition of the relevant parameters and key terms.

The concluding paragraph draws together the main arguments and links to the main contention stated in the introductory paragraph. Having substantiated the arguments in the body, you can now summarise the key ideas and confirm the validity of the position you have taken. Within this concluding paragraph you may explore the implications of your premise and/or confirm the scope and limitations of your argument without introducing any new information. In the final sentences, reference is usually made to the question/topic; however, you might consider including a rhetorical question, a thought-provoking quotation or a powerful statement to challenge the reader.

After completing your draft, step away from your writing so that you can return with a refreshed perspective. The initial drafting phase is an intense process and can be mentally and physically tiring. Taking a break will restore you and enable you to return to the next phase with renewed vigour.

Connecting sentences

As a writer, you might think that your job is done once you have written down all the basic ideas. This is not the case! A reader needs to see the *connections* between your ideas too. Tell the reader how each sentence is related to the next. Writing is not like speaking, so the reader cannot ask you what you meant if they misunderstand what you have written. Read the following paragraphs. Can they be made even better?

> *Families that communicate effectively transmit messages clearly. Members are free to express their feelings without fear of jeopardising their standing in the family. Family members can support one another and have the ability to listen, empathise, and reach out to one another in times of crisis. They are more able to reach out to meet the needs of others in society.*
>
> *Messages are often communicated unclearly when patterns of communication among family members are dysfunctional. Verbal*

communication may be incongruent with nonverbal messages. Power struggles may be evidenced by hostility, anger, or silence. Members may be cautious in expressing their feelings. They cannot predict how others in the family will respond. The growth of individual members is stunted. Members often turn to other systems to seek personal validation and gratification. (passage adapted from Berman et al., 2012, p. 495)

Help the reader by 'signposting' the connections between your sentences. Think about it: when you see a word like 'however' you immediately know a contradictory idea is coming up.

Let's glue some of the above sentences together using the connecting words found in **Table 3.2**.

Families that communicate effectively transmit messages clearly. _____, members are free to express their feelings without fear of jeopardising their standing in the family. _____, family members can support one another and have the ability to listen, empathise, and reach out to one another in times of crisis. _____, they are more able to reach out to meet the needs of others in society.

_____, messages are often communicated unclearly when patterns of communication among family members are dysfunctional. _____, verbal communication may be incongruent with nonverbal messages. Power struggles may be evidenced by hostility, anger, or silence. _____, members may be cautious in expressing their feelings _____ they cannot predict how others in the family will respond. _____, the growth of individual members is stunted. _____, members often turn to other systems to seek personal validation and gratification.

Berman, A., Snyder, S. J., Levette-Jones, T., Dwyer, T., Hales, M., Harvey, N., ... Stanley, D. (Eds.). (2012). *Kozier & Erb's fundamentals of nursing* (2nd Australian ed., vol. 1). Frenchs Forest, NSW: Pearson Australia.

Table 3.2 Connecting sentences

Addition	apart from this, as well as, besides, furthermore, in addition, moreover, nor, not only … but also, too, what is more
Cause and effect	accordingly, as a consequence, as a result, because (of this), consequently, for this reason, hence, in order to, owing to this, so, so that, therefore, this leads to, thus
Comparison/similar ideas	in comparison, in the same way, likewise, similarly
Condition	if, in that case, provided that, unless
Contradiction	actually, as a matter of fact, in fact
Contrast/opposite ideas	although, but, despite, in spite of, even so, however, in contrast, in spite of this, nevertheless, on the contrary, on the other hand, whereas, yet
Emphasis	chiefly, especially, importantly, indeed, in detail, in particular, mainly, notably, particularly
Examples	for example, for instance, such as, thus, as follows
Explanation/equivalence	in other words, namely, or rather, this means, to be more precise
Generalisation	as a rule, for the most part, generally, in general, normally, on the whole, in most cases, usually
Stating the obvious	clearly, naturally, obviously, surely
Summary/conclusion	finally, in brief, in conclusion, in short, in summary, overall, to conclude
Support	actually, as a matter of fact, in fact, indeed
Time/order	at first, eventually, finally, first(ly), in the first/second place, initially, lastly, later, next, prior to, second(ly)

* Note: a comma is frequently used after a connecting word, e.g. 'In comparison, …'

Gillett, A., Hammond, A., & Martala, M. (2009). *Inside track to successful academic writing*. Harlow, England: Pearson Education Ltd.

5. Edit

Taking a break after completing the initial draft allows you to approach this next phase, editing, with greater objectivity and clarity. This will enable you to reflect on your unique academic writing style, identify obvious errors and discrepancies in your argument, and creatively re-craft your words to express yourself in a more informative and engaging way.

The purpose of editing is to objectively evaluate the content and logic of your argument, and the structure and style of the writing. High-quality writing is the result of a reflective and thorough editing process. Consequently, if you want to achieve a high standard in your academic writing, you will need to focus on editing and refining your first draft of each individual paragraph, as well as the introductory and concluding paragraphs, prior to revising the overall work.

Consider the aspects set out in Table 3.3 with regards to overall content and structure.

Table 3.3 Overall content and structure

Have you addressed the complexities of the question/topic?
Does the first paragraph provide the framework for the body of writing?
Does the body explore the arguments sequentially in relation to the introduction?
Has the concluding paragraph captured the essence of the position taken?
Is there consistency in the position you have taken?
Are there any repetitious ideas or statements?
Have you overused any words or phrases?
Are there any obvious omissions?
Has every source been referenced in your text?

6. Proofread

Editing and proofreading are related but serve different purposes. While editing concentrates on the macro aspects of your writing (content, clarity, logic and structure), proofreading takes a more detailed or micro view: it can be likened to looking at your writing through a magnifying glass. This is where you consider and fine-tune the consistency in spelling, vocabulary, grammar and punctuation. In an academic environment, as well as in the workplace, application of these basic structures of written language is highly valued as it demonstrates an attention to detail, diligence, and commitment to a high standard of work.

Spelling

The purpose of correct spelling is to ensure that your meaning is clear and unambiguous, and that the words do not interrupt the flow of your ideas and distract the reader.

> Use a dictionary (in preference to relying on the computer spellcheck function).
> Check both spelling and meaning; if you are unsure of how to spell a word, ask someone who may know.
> Ensure the word you have chosen is appropriate to the context.
> Select words you understand.

Vocabulary

The choice of vocabulary in academic writing influences the tone of your writing. As you read more widely, you will enrich and expand your vocabulary and have available a more comprehensive selection of words. You will also develop a technical and specific vocabulary pertinent to your discipline area. Each of these factors will inform your writing; however, it is important to ensure you understand and can use new words effectively and in context.

> Use a thesaurus and a dictionary.
> Understand each word you use.
> Read widely.
> Select words which convey your message.

Grammar

Grammar forms the technical structure for language. Meaning is evident through the construction of sentences that comply with the grammatical rules of language. For example, in English, every sentence must contain at least one verb and one noun. Applying the grammatical rules will enable you to construct meaningful sentences.

> Vary the beginnings of sentences and avoid repetition.
> Modify the length of your sentences – sentences which are too long lose meaning; conversely, sentences which are too short inhibit the flow of ideas.
> Connect or list similar ideas or concepts together to facilitate meaning.
> Consider the arrangement of the phrases to ensure a logical or chronological progression.
> Select words and craft sentences to communicate your ideas succinctly.
> Express your ideas in a positive tone – this enhances understanding and engages the reader.
> Use conjunctions to join ideas within a sentence.

> Use connective words to link ideas in different sentences.

> Consider carefully the use of active and passive voice in your writing.

> Understand the rules of grammar and apply them to your own work in preference to relying on the computer grammar check.

Punctuation

Punctuation provides the vital tools needed to construct a grammatical sentence. Punctuation such as full stops, commas, colons, hyphens, apostrophes, and capital letters are signals which define meaning in a sentence. Consider the following paragraph:

> *because of their unique position in the health care system nurses experience conflicts between their loyalties and obligations to clients families primary care providers employing institutions and licensing bodies client needs may conflict with institutional policies primary care provider preferences needs of the clients family or even laws of the state according to the nursing code of ethics the nurses first loyalty is to the client* mcpherson & stakenberg 2012 p 96.

Misplaced punctuation or no punctuation will dramatically change the meaning of a sentence and leave it open to misinterpretation or ambiguity. Now consider the paragraph when punctuated correctly:

> *Because of their unique position in the health care system, nurses experience conflicts between their loyalties and obligations to clients, families, primary care providers, employing institutions, and licensing bodies. Client needs may conflict with institutional policies, primary care provider preferences, needs of the client's family, or even laws of the state. According to the nursing code of ethics, the nurse's first loyalty is to the client* (McPherson & Stakenberg, 2012, p. 96).

Use the following tips to assist in proofreading for punctuation:

> It might help to proofread for one aspect of writing at a time. For example: on the first scan, check each sentence structure; on the next scan, check your verbs; on the next scan, check your use of vocabulary; and so on.

> Use punctuation to group similar ideas – for example, a list.

> Refer to a grammar reference book or search online for grammar support.

> Use learning support staff for advice on how to use punctuation correctly.

Commas

Commas are sometimes troublesome to learners of English because they are used differently in other languages. There are many comma rules in English, but you may remember them more easily if you realise that they can be organised into just four main groups: **introducers, coordinators, inserters,** and **tags.** Each group of commas relates to independent clauses in a particular way, except the coordinator group. Coordinator commas link not just independent clauses but *any* coordinate (equal) elements in a sentence.

Study the examples for each comma group, and notice the kinds of elements that can be introducers, coordinators, inserters, and tags.

Introducer Commas

An introducer comma follows any element that comes in front of the first independent clause in a sentence.

Words	*Therefore, I plan to quit smoking.* *Nervously, I threw away my cigarettes.*
Phrases	*As a result, I feel terrible right now.* *After 16 years of smoking, it is not easy to quit.* *Having smoked for 16 years, I find it difficult to quit.*
Dependent clauses	*Because I have a chronic cough, my doctor recommended that I quit immediately.*
Direct quotations	*"Stop smoking today," she advised.*

Coordinator Commas

Together with a coordinating conjunction, a comma links coordinate (equal) elements in a sentence.

Compound sentence with 2 independent clauses	*She has a good job, yet she is always broke.* *They were tired, so they went home early.*
Series of 3 or more words	*He does not enjoy **skiing, ice-skating,** or **sledding.*** *Cecille speaks **English, Spanish, French,** and **Creole.***
	(No comma with only two items: Chen speaks Mandarin and Taiwanese.)

*A nurse has to work **at night, on weekends,** and **on holidays.*** *We **ran into the airport, checked our luggage, raced to the boarding gate, gave the attendant our boarding passes,** and **collapsed in our seats.***

Inserter Commas

An inserter comma is used before and after any element that is inserted into the middle of an independent clause.

Words *My uncle, **however,** refuses to quit smoking.*

Phrases *My father, **on the other hand,** has never smoked.* *There is no point in living, **according to my uncle,** if you do not do what you enjoy.*

Nonrestrictive phrases and clauses *My aunt, **his wife,** died of lung cancer.* *My cousins, **grieving over their mother's death,** resolved never to smoke.* *My mother, **who just celebrated her fiftieth birthday,** enjoys an occasional cigarette.*

Reporting verbs in direct quotations: *"I have tried to quit dozens of times," **she says,** "but I can't."*

Tag Commas

A tag comma is used when adding certain elements to the end of a sentence.

Words *My uncle believes in drinking a daily glass of wine, **too.*** *He appears to be in good health, **however.***

Phrases *He swims for an hour every day, **for example.*** *He also plays tennis, **beating me most of the time.***

Tag questions *It is not logical, **is it?***

Direct quotations *He laughs as he says, **"I will outlive all of you."***

Recognising comma splices

When you edit your writing, look carefully at sentences that contain commas. Does the sentence contain two main clauses? If so, are the main clauses joined by a comma and coordinating conjunction (*for, and, nor, but, or, yet, so*)?

Incorrect   The concept of 'nature' depends on the concept of human 'culture', the problem is that 'culture' is itself shaped by 'nature'. [Two main clauses joined by only a comma]

Correct   Even though the concept of 'nature' depends on the concept of human 'culture', 'culture' is itself shaped by 'nature'. [Subordinate clause plus a main clause]

Correct   The concept of 'nature' depends on the concept of human 'culture', but 'culture' is itself shaped by 'nature'. [Two main clauses joined by a comma and coordinating conjunction]

The word *however* produces some of the most common comma splice errors. *However* usually functions to begin a main clause, and when it does it should be preceded by a semicolon rather than a comma. However, when 'however' appears at the beginning of a sentence, it is incorrect to precede it with a semicolon. Some students, however, like to use 'however' as an interrupter. In this case, it is bracketed by commas.

Incorrect   The foreign affairs minister repeatedly vowed that the government wasn't choosing a side between the two countries embroiled in conflict, however the developing foreign policy suggested otherwise.

Correct   The foreign affairs minister repeatedly vowed that the government wasn't choosing a side between the two countries embroiled in conflict; however, the developing foreign policy suggested otherwise. [Two main clauses joined by a semicolon]

Remember: Don't use a comma as a full stop.

Recognising run-on sentences

When you read this sentence, you realise something is wrong.

I don't recall what kind of printer it was all I remember is that it could sort, staple and print a packet at the same time.

The problem is that two main clauses aren't separated by punctuation. The reader must look carefully to determine where one main clause stops and the next one begins.

I don't recall what kind of printer it was | all I remember is that it could sort, staple and print a packet at the same time.

The most common way to correct this run-on is to place a full stop after *was*, and then begin the next sentence with a capital letter:

I don't recall what kind of printer it was. All I remember is that it could sort, staple and print a packet at the same time.

Run-on sentences are major errors because they force the reader to re-read the sentence in order to understand it.

Remember: Two main clauses must be separated by correct punctuation.

Recognising fragments

If you can spot fragments, you can fix them. Grammar checkers can find some of them, but they miss many fragments and may incorrectly identify other sentences as fragments. Ask these questions when you are checking for sentence fragments.

- **Does the sentence have a subject?** Except for commands, sentences need subjects:

  Jane spent every cent of credit she had available. And then applied for more cards.

- **Does the sentence have a complete verb?** Sentences require complete verbs. Verbs that end in *-ing* must have an auxiliary verb to be complete.

  Robert keeps changing courses. He trying to figure out what he really wants to do after university.

- **If the sentence begins with a subordinate clause, is there a main clause in the same sentence?**

  Even though it is cheaper to watch a DVD than visit a movie theatre, it is the total experience that moviegoers enjoy. Which is one reason people continue to go to the movies.

Remember:
1. A sentence must have a subject and a complete verb.
2. A subordinate clause cannot stand alone as a sentence.

Faulty parallel structure

When writers neglect to use parallel structure, the result can be jarring. Reading your writing aloud will help you catch problems in parallelism. Read this sentence aloud:

  At our club meeting we identified problems in finding new members, publicising our activities and **maintenance** of our website.

The end of the sentence doesn't sound right because the parallel structure is broken. We expect to find another verb + *ing* following *finding* and *publicising*. Instead, we run into *maintenance*, a noun. The problem is easy to fix: change the noun to the *-ing* verb form.

  At our club meeting we identified problems in finding new members, publicising our activities and maintaining our website.

Remember: Use parallel structure for parallel ideas.

Dangling modifiers

A dangling modifier doesn't seem to modify anything in a sentence; it dangles, unconnected to the word or words it presumably is intended to modify. Frequently, it produces funny results:

> I saw four kangaroos driving down the road.

It sounds as if *the kangaroos* were driving. The problem is that the subject, *I*, is missing:

> I saw four kangaroos while I was driving down the road.

Remember: Modifiers should be clearly connected to the words they modify, especially at the beginning of sentences.

Agreement errors using *each*

When a pronoun is singular, its verb must be singular. A common stumbling block to this rule is the pronoun *each*. *Each* is always treated as a singular pronoun in academic writing. When *each* stands alone, the choice is easy to make:

| Incorrect | **Each** are an outstanding student. |
| Correct | **Each** is an outstanding student. |

But when *each* is modified by a phrase that includes a plural noun, the choice of a singular verb form becomes less obvious:

Incorrect	**Each** of the girls are fit.
Correct	**Each** of the girls is fit.
Incorrect	**Each** of our dogs get a present.
Correct	**Each** of our dogs gets a present.

Remember: *Each* is always singular.

Collective nouns as subjects

Collective nouns refer to groups (*audience*, *class*, *committee*, *crowd*, *family*, *government*, *group*, *jury*, *public*, *team*). When members of a group are considered as a unit, use singular verbs and singular pronouns.

> The **crowd** is unusually quiet at the moment, but it will get noisy soon.

When members of a group are considered as individuals, use plural verbs and plural pronouns.

> The **staff** have **their** differing opinions on how to address the problems caused by reduced government support.

Sometimes collective nouns can be singular in one context and plural in another. Writers must decide which verb form to use based on sentence context.

> The **number** of people who live in the inner city is increasing.

> A **number** of people are moving into the inner city from the suburbs.

Indefinite pronouns

Indefinite pronouns (such as *anybody*, *anything*, *each*, *either*, *everybody*, *everything*, *neither*, *none*, *somebody*, *something*) refer to unspecified people or things. Most take singular pronouns.

Incorrect	Everybody can choose their flatmates.
Correct	Everybody can choose his or her flatmate.
Correct alternative	All students can choose their flatmates.

A few indefinite pronouns (*all*, *any*, *either*, *more*, *most*, *neither*, *none*, *some*) can take either singular or plural pronouns.

Correct	**Some** of the shipment was damaged when it became overheated.
Correct	**All** thought they should have a good seat at the concert.

A few pronouns are always plural (*few*, *many, several*).

Correct	**Several** want refunds.

Remember: Words that begin with *any*, *some* and *every* are usually singular.

Unnecessary tense shift

Notice the tense shift in the following example.

Incorrect   On census night 2016, a cyber attack **crippled** [PAST TENSE] the Australian Bureau of Statistics web server and **irritated** [PAST TENSE] millions of Australians. As the attack **threatens** [PRESENT TENSE] security and **inconveniences** [PRESENT TENSE] millions of people, the Bureau **is** [PRESENT TENSE] forced to shut down its web site.

The second sentence shifts unnecessarily to the present tense, confusing the reader. Did the Australian Bureau of Statistics shut down the server in the past, or is it doing this now? Changing the verbs in the second sentence to the past tense eliminates the confusion.

Correct   On census night 2016, a cyber attack **crippled** [PAST TENSE] the Australian Bureau of Statistics web server and **irritated** [PAST TENSE] millions of Australians. As the attack **threatened** [PAST TENSE] security and **inconvenienced** [PAST TENSE] millions of people, the Bureau **was** [PAST TENSE] forced to shut down its web site.

Remember: Shift verb tense only when you are referring to different time periods.

After you have proofread your own work, ask someone else to read it as they will read it with an objective view and identify errors you may have missed.

Alternatively, try reading your work backwards from right to left to pick up spelling errors, repeated words and unnecessary punctuation. As the author, you can become too familiar with your own work and may gloss over the finer details. This unusual approach provides you with an unfamiliar perspective and therefore a more objective point of view.

In academic writing, you are required to incorporate the ideas of others in your own work; therefore, when you proofread, it is essential to check that you have acknowledged and referenced all your sources of information and that the reference style you have used is applied consistently and accurately.

> Check the marking criteria
> Allow enough time to plan and write
> Build on what you already know
> Research thoroughly
> Record all sources

Chapter summary

Writing in an academic environment requires an understanding of a variety of structures: report, essay and case studies, as discussed in Chapter 2. However, in academia a high standard and style of writing is expected. This necessitates a conscientious and diligent approach to writing where you will need to: analyse the question or topic; carry out research; develop a plan; write a first draft; edit and proofread, in order to create a thought-provoking and well-structured academic work. Through this process, and as you read widely in your discipline area, your writing skills will evolve and you will become more confident in writing in an academic style.

Summary activities

1. Define and use these words in meaningful sentences:
   Cognitive
   Slang
   Ambiguity
   Analyse
   Idiom
   Evaluate
   Synopsis
   Pragmatic
2. Brainstorm and construct a concept map related to this topic:
   Australia needs a sustainable population strategy. Debate the impacts of this.
3. Develop a writing plan using the concept map and your research as the framework – refer back to Figure 3.6 on page 114.
4. Develop a draft essay using your writing plan for this topic:
   Australia needs a sustainable population strategy. Debate the impacts of this.
5. Review your draft using the editing guide questions on p. 131 and in Tables 2.6, and 3.3.

Reflection

How did the editing guide questions enable you to present a clear and well-structured piece of writing?

Photo credits

4 Acknowledge Others!

Refer to others within your writing

Learning Outcomes

By the end of this chapter you will have strategies which enable you to:

> manage and evaluate references from a range of sources
> quote, paraphrase and summarise from an original source
> use in-text citation using appropriate referencing style
> apply appropriate techniques to avoid plagiarism and collusion
> select and apply cognitive strategies to assist research
> establish academic integrity by acknowledging original sources.

In academia, it is assumed you will encompass and draw on the work and knowledge of others in order to support and validate your premise. You will be expected to read from a wide range of resources which will involve you in current and past academic discussions within your discipline. These sources of information may include academic journals, texts, reference books, conference papers, reports, lectures and online databases. It is vitally important that you maintain your academic integrity and preserve the intellectual property of others through the use of a referencing system. Correct in-text citation and the use of a reference list to record full referencing details are integral parts of an academic research process and imperative to your success at university.

What is referencing?

Referencing is a formalised system for acknowledging the work of others in your own academic work. When you reference a source in your writing by citing bibliographic details you use a form of referencing known as **citation**.

Why reference?

Fundamentally, referencing is used to acknowledge an author's original work. There is a global understanding that all authors are entitled to respect and credit for their intellectual property, which is generally protected by the laws of copyright. Intellectual property encompasses ideas, theories, hypotheses, research findings, images, graphs, diagrams, statistics, charts and illustrations, all of which may be used in academic writing if acknowledged correctly through citation. At university, it is expected that through research, analysis and evaluation, you will incorporate the ideas of others in your work, engage in ongoing academic discussion, and enter into the current oral and written debates in your field of study. However, it is essential that you acknowledge all sources cited regardless of whether you have rephrased the ideas in your own words. The techniques for legally incorporating the ideas of others in your own writing – including quoting, summarising and paraphrasing, with accurate citations – are demonstrated and explained later in this chapter.

Referencing encompasses a range of purposes. It is used to:

> acknowledge the intellectual property of others – and avoid plagiarism
> explore theoretical perspectives to endorse your premise
> validate your statements or conclusions with the application of theory and to substantiate with evidence
> demonstrate the scope of your reading and research
> enable the reader to locate and verify the original sources mentioned in your writing
> enable the reader to engage in the academic discussion by reading further
> permit the reader to examine the original source and check the accuracy of direct quotations, paraphrases or summaries cited in your work
> allow the marker to ascertain whether cited information has been fully understood and incorporated in the correct and appropriate context.

'Education is the most powerful weapon which you can use to change the world.' —*Nelson Mandela*

Some tips for selecting references

- Try to find references which are less than 5 years old, and usually no older than 10 years – keep your nursing evidence up to date!
- It is common to have 5 or more quality references per 1,000 words, since nursing is evidence-based.
- Use reputable sources! (See pp. 186–205, the chapter on reading critically.) Find peer-reviewed and authoritative sources such as refereed journals, books, and institutional publications. Avoid newspapers, unreferenced generic health websites, online health encyclopedias/dictionaries and non-institutional websites.

Plagiarism

All ideas, theories and findings are the original work of the person who first created them. When you incorporate the research of others into your own body of work, it is vital that you are ethically responsible and acknowledge those authors in order to avoid plagiarism. When the intellectual property of others is *not* acknowledged in work which you claim to be your own, you are plagiarising. Technically, plagiarism amounts to fraud, even theft, and is regarded as a serious infringement. Complying with the citation or referencing style guides will enable you to avoid plagiarism; you will maintain your academic integrity, have a clear sense of what is your work and what belongs to someone else, and gain a sense of satisfaction in creating an original perspective.

As you research, you will notice the way in which authors of academic work cite the sources of research and theories. Citing sources demonstrates respect for the authors who have researched and formulated their own concepts and original ideas, and also identifies the process by which new knowledge is obtained and expanded. In your academic work you will necessarily take from a range of concepts formulated by others. By incorporating and citing the previous knowledge in your own work, you build on it to construct your own point of view which then becomes *your* original concept. In this way you have acknowledged the input of other authors to your work whilst generating your own contribution to academic discussion. This is a constructivist approach to your learning. Understanding the concept of *why* referencing is so important is fundamental to accurate citation.

The following example is a direct citation taken from Bradshaw et al. (2012, p. 13).

Nurses assume a number of roles when they provide person-centred care to clients. Nurses often carry out these roles concurrently not exclusively of one another. For example, the nurse may act as a counsellor while providing physical care and teaching aspects of that care. (Bradshaw, 2012, p. 13)

The example below demonstrates plagiarism. Merely changing some of the words and the order in which they are written does not alter the fact that these ideas and words are the original work of Bradshaw et al. (2012) and consequently must be acknowledged as the original source using correct citation.

Nurses play a number of roles when they care for clients. Nurses frequently do these roles concurrently and not separately of one another. For example, the nurse may be a counsellor while providing physical activities and the educational aspects of that care.

To avoid plagiarism, the above text can be used with the correct citation as shown below:

As a part of person-centred care, nurses may need to fulfil a number of roles. Bradshaw (2012, p. 13) writes that these roles are often required "concurrently, not exclusively of one another". She gives an example of this by pointing out that the nurse who gives physical care may be required to counsel the patient while they work on the client, and take the opportunity to provide education whenever they can (Bradshaw, 2012, p. 13).

Plagiarism is avoidable. Once you know the strategies for citing correctly, dependent on the style of referencing required, you may legally incorporate the ideas and theories of others into your work to support your premise or to substantiate the purpose of your writing. The following list provides general strategies for citing effectively:

> Adhere to the APA (6th edition) referencing style guide and your topic details.
> Ensure you know the original source of the material you incorporate.
> Use quotation marks and acknowledge the source whenever you incorporate the *exact* words of another person in your own work.
> Use correct citation when you use your own words to paraphrase or summarise another's work.
> Acknowledge all forms of reference sources (written and spoken words, theories, ideas, facts, tables, charts, pictures, conference proceedings, company

reports and brochures, electronic articles, newspapers, journals) in the text, and provide the full referencing details in the reference list.

Table 4.1 Plagiarism in academic writing

If you find any of the following problems in your academic writing, you may be guilty of plagiarising someone else's work. Because plagiarism is usually inadvertent, it is especially important that you understand what constitutes using sources responsibly. Avoid these pitfalls.

- **Missing attribution.** Make sure the author of a quotation has been identified. Include a lead-in or signal phrase that provides attribution to the source, and identify the author in the citation.
- **Missing quotation marks.** You must put quotation marks around words quoted directly from a source.
- **Inadequate citation.** Give a page number to show where in the source the quotation appears or where a paraphrase or summary is drawn from.
- **Paraphrase relies too heavily on the source.** Be careful that the wording or sentence structure of a paraphrase does not follow the source too closely.
- **Distortion of meaning.** Don't allow your paraphrase or summary to distort the meaning of the source, and don't take a quotation out of context, resulting in a change of meaning.
- **Missing works-cited entry.** The Works-Cited page or References page must include all the works cited in the project.
- **Inadequate citation of images.** A figure or photo must appear with a caption and a citation to indicate the source of the image. If material includes a summary of data from a visual source, an attribution or citation must be given for the graphic being summarised.

Collusion

At university, secretly agreeing with another student and making a conscious decision to share or copy a piece of work for submission is regarded as a serious offence and is known as collusion. **Collusion** encompasses any deliberate act of deception to gain an advantage in your academic study. Whilst in an academic environment students are encouraged to work collaboratively in study groups to share and explore ideas, there is the expectation that all students will submit work that is uniquely theirs.

Acts of collusion may include:

> submitting a past student's assignment
> borrowing paragraphs or excerpts from another person's work (even with permission)

> inadvertently using similar sentence constructions to express the same ideas which may occur unconsciously as a result of working closely with a fellow student.

As a study group, formulate rules and boundaries for sharing information and resources to avoid inadvertent collusion.

> Maintaining your academic honesty and integrity is paramount to your success at university. A high ethical standard is expected from all students and staff. Strategies for avoiding collusion and plagiarism begin with an understanding and awareness of these concepts.

Be aware that there are software tools used by markers to detect plagiarised text in academic environments.

Academic integrity

All students should be familiar with the website 'Academic integrity at Flinders', available in FLO https://flo.flinders.edu.au/course/view.php?id=104. It contains defintions of academic integrity and an explanation of its importance, and tips on how to avoid plagiarism, collusion, or being accused of academic dishonesty. Find out more about the university's policies relating to academic integrity: The Student Academic Integrity Procedures policy https://www.flinders.edu.au/content/dam/documents/staff/policies/academic-students/student-academic-integrity-procedures.pdf and the Student Academic Integrity Policy https://www.flinders.edu.au/content/dam/documents/staff/policies/academic-students/student-academic-integrity-policy.pdf are important documents to familiarise yourself with.

When to reference

In order to fulfil the purposes of referencing and avoid plagiarism and collusion, it is essential to provide reference details for each source in a format consistent with the prescribed reference style. Each and every source used to support your work must be referenced, including information accessed from the World Wide Web, tables, figures, diagrams, appendices, written and spoken words, theories, ideas, facts, conference proceedings, reports and journals. The citation of references in your work is incorporated in two ways: in-text citations and reference lists.

Using in-text citations allows you to legally integrate the work of others to support and provide evidence for your premise within the body of your work. This is where you express the information in your own words and use direct quotations. The process of citing incorporates the ability to quote, paraphrase and summarise the work of others with consideration to the quality, quantity, context and relevance of the citation to your premise. See Table 4.2 which compares the major features of each of these forms of citations.

Compiling a reference list at the conclusion of your work is the second method of citation. The reference list contains all the details of each source quoted, paraphrased or summarised *within* your work.

How to reference

In-text

Quote

Referring to another author's written or spoken work using the exact words is known as quoting. When you quote directly from a source, you must provide correct reference details (citation). A direct quotation can be a powerful tool in your academic writing or presentations, particularly in the following cases:

> The original writer's ideas are expressed in a significant and influential way.
  'The providers of health care, also referred to as the health care team or health professionals, are nurses and health personnel from different disciplines who coordinate their skills to assist clients and their support persons' (Gonda & Hales, 2012, p. 115)

> It is used to explain or define a term from a respected authority, to compare and contrast, or to elaborate further.
  The Nursing and Midwifery Board of Australia (NMBA) provides guidelines on 'the responsibilities for which nurses are accountable and provide for the practice of nursing regardless of the area of specialisation' (Bradshaw, 2012, p. 12).

> Tables, graphs or pictures from a respected authority are included to support your premise and illustrate an argument or position. (See Figure 4.1.)

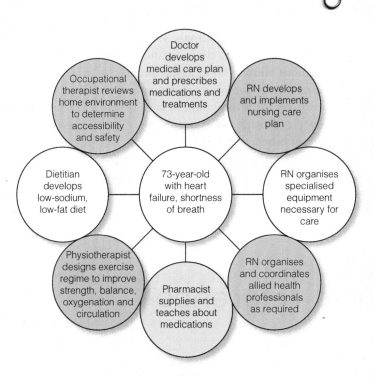

Figure 4.1 An example of a health care team and their responsibilities (Gonda & Hales 2012, p. 116)

When inserting a direct quotation, introduce it with an explanatory sentence to ensure its meaning and impact is not compromised; this demonstrates your understanding of the author's statement and its relevance to your premise. It will be clear to the reader that the quoted words are not yours but those of the original author, because you will cite the source using the appropriate reference style.

> *A registered nurse (RN) plays an important role in the assessment of a client's status and coordinating care on a daily basis. However, it is possible that an enrolled nurse (EN) may assist in the 'direct client care under the direction of an RN' (Gonda & Hales, 2012, p. 115).*

In your choice of quotations there may be words that do not add meaning to your context. Occasionally omitting words might provide a greater impact; however, carefully consider which words to omit, to ensure the meaning and relevance of the quotation is not compromised. Always remember that you are quoting directly from an author's original work. Consequently, it is necessary to indicate to the reader that you are using only part of a sentence by inserting an ellipsis. An **ellipsis** is a series of three full stops separated by one space each, used to mark the omission of words.

> *Another kind of nurse is advanced practice nurses (APNs). The APNs 'have certifications that ... may allow to provide primary care, prescribe medications and make referrals' (Gonda & Hales, 2012, p. 115).*

The author–date reference guide will provide directions as to how to include a direct quotation in a text. The guide will also specify the formatting style to be adopted when inserting quotations into your assignments.

Choose a quotation carefully, and introduce it with an explanatory sentence to ensure its meaning and retain its impact.

Paraphrase

Paraphrasing is the preferred method for incorporating the work of others into your composition, as this demonstrates your understanding and application of the idea, concept or theory. The process of describing and discussing information from another source is called paraphrasing and requires you to rephrase an original work using your words and phrases. Despite presenting the information using different words, the written or spoken text remains the intellectual property of the original author and must be acknowledged using correct citation.

Rephrasing an original idea into your own words requires careful consideration, which begins with determining the relevance of an original piece to your purpose. Consider the following questions when making a decision to paraphrase a particular spoken or written text:

> Do you understand the text?
> Would it support or validate your premise?
> How will it add meaning to your argument?
> Do you have a clear purpose for including the text?
> Does the text provide a point of interest which enhances your work?
> Can the text be used to emphasise your position?
> How does the text provide evidence to reinforce your position?

Prior to paraphrasing the text you have selected, determine how much of the text to incorporate and then paraphrase it using a similar number of words to the original. Paraphrasing passages which are either too large or too small may jeopardise the impact and meaning of the reference. Use paraphrases discreetly to reinforce your position, rather than taking a piecemeal approach and connecting a number of paraphrased sources without a clear rationale.

Steps for successful paraphrasing

- Read the original source and determine its relevance.
- Check the meanings of words.
- Place the original out of sight.
- List the main points in your own words.
- Re-read the original and check that you have included all the main points.
- Put the original away again.
- Draft a sentence or paragraph around the main points.
- Ensure that you do not misinterpret or change the original meaning.
- Write in a style and language that is indicative of you.
- Alter the sentence structure by changing grammar, punctuation and verb tenses.
- Use synonyms **judiciously**.

Paraphrase the following paragraph:

Nurses use critical thinking and judgement to collect and interpret the most relevant information needed to make decisions. Nurses must use good judgement, for example, to decide which observations must be reported to the physician immediately and which can be noted in the client record for the physician to address later, during a routine visit with the client. Given that nurses have a high level of patient contact, they have an important role in the overall decision-making process involved in the care of the patient. (Scully, 2012, p. 197)

Identify the key words and paraphrase the following text:

Scully (2012, p. 197) explains that nurses make important decisions using critical thinking and interpretation. These decisions are based upon the identification and collection of pertinent information. An illustration of this need for good decision making is when nurses make their regular patient observations and they must judge whether they need to report what they find to the physician immediately or later through the patient's records (Scully, 2012, p. 197). Arguably, due to their frequent regular contact and oberservation of patients, the nurse is a key player in forming care-based decisions.

Summarise

A summary encapsulates the essence of an author's original work. It is a précis of an original work containing the main ideas rephrased in your words and cited appropriately. Whilst there is a correlation between the length of a paraphrase and the original text, there is no such restriction for a summary. The length and detail of it will depend upon your understanding of the original text and your purpose for creating the summary. At times it may be adequate to summarise in one sentence the theme of a chapter or article, or the hypothesis of a thesis or research, providing it accurately sums up the original text.

Strategies for writing a summary:

1. Be selective and use information relevant to the topic.
2. Condense the text to identify the main points and omit the details.
3. Use fewer words than the original text.
4. Only include the author's ideas.

Read the following original text:

Postural draining is the use of positioning techniques that promotes the movement of secretions from specific segments of the lungs and bronchi into the trachea. Coughing or suctioning normally removes secretions from the trachea. The procedure for postural drainage can include most lung segments. Because patients may not require postural drainage of all lung segments, the procedure is based on clinical assessment findings. For example, patients with left lower lobe atelectasis may require postural drainage of only the affected region, whereas a child with cystic fibrosis may require postural drainage of all lung segments (Crisp & Taylor, 2009, p. 982).

A suggested summary of the above paragraph follows:

Postural draining involves positioning the body in ways that mobilise secretions out of the lungs and bronchi in preparation for either coughing or suctioning, and postural draining procedures vary according to patient need (Crisp & Taylor, 2009, p. 982).

It is useful to note that when inserting a summarised source in your work, you introduce the summary using reporting verbs such as *proposes*, *contends*, *hypothesises*, *states*, *compares*, and *suggests*. For example:

The devastating impact of poverty on health outcomes has been examined by . . . in their study of . . .

Table 4.2 Comparative table

Feature	Quotation	Paraphrase	Summary
Size	Phrases, clauses or a few significant sentences	Generally relates to a sentence or two of original text but no more than a paragraph	May be as small as a paragraph or chapter, or may be a summary of an entire book
Content	Exact replica of the original text	Restates the spoken or written text in your words	Restates only the main ideas in your words
Structure	Matches the source word-for-word	Is similar in length to the original text	May be as detailed or brief as required
Meaning	Is the original meaning	Replicates the original meaning of the text	Is an overview of the text
In-text format	Appears between quotation marks	Introduced using reporting verbs	Introduced using reporting verbs
Citation	Includes appropriate citation	Includes appropriate citation	Includes appropriate citation

CVC dressing

The dressing for a central venous catheter (CVC) can be semi-permeable transparent or a gauze dressing. Transparent dressings ensure the insertion site is visible, may require fewer changes, secure the catheter and permit the patient to bathe or shower without saturating the dressing. The disadvantages are they are more expensive than gauze dressings, are difficult to apply to a diaphoretic patient, and may allow moisture to accumulate, which can increase the opportunity to micro-organisms to be transmitted. The advantages of dry gauze dressings are that they absorb moisture and are less expensive, although the insertion site is not visible and needs to be changed more frequently. If the patient is diaphoretic, or if the site is bleeding, a gauze dressing is preferred. Otherwise, use either a transparent dressing alone or a gauze dressing with tape. A combination of dressing types is not recommended because a gauze dressing covered with a transparent dressing can harbour moisture and provide an environment for bacterial growth. The decision about which dressing to use is made on its ability to provide a protective barrier, keep the skin at the insertion site dry, secure the catheter, and decrease the risk of colonisation by micro-organisms.

(This text is adapted and copied from: Tollefson, J. (2012). *Clinical psychomotor skills: Assessment tools for nursing students* (5th ed., p. 98). South Melbourne, Australia: Cengage Learning.

How will you decide when to use a quotation, paraphrase or summary to legally integrate the work of others in your own work?

How will you decide which of the three techniques to use?

Please answer the following questions

1. How would you reference this in the main body of your writing? Create an **in-text citation**.

(you may need to look at the next chapter for some hints on how to do this, and don't forget to use the page number)

2. Please finish this sentence with a **direct quote** from the text, and use in-text citation.

The two types of dressing should not be used at the same time because

_____

_____

_____

3. Please paraphrase by combining the first and last sentences of the paragraph, and use in-text citation.

_____

_____

_____

4. Please summarise the main points of this paragraph, using only one or two sentences, and use in-text citation.

_____

_____

_____

Planning oral medication administration

The administration of oral medications requires some planning. Position the patient to facilitate administering the medication. Most patients prefer to sit upright to swallow medications. If that position is impossible, the patient should be positioned for safety and comfort – for example, lying on their side rather than supine. Assessing the patient for ability to sit, swallow, and follow instructions is important to assure their safety. Some medications require assessment of the patient prior to administration. Examples are a respiratory assessment prior to administering a bronchodilator in an asthmatic patient, fluid balance for a patient receiving diuretics, apical pulse assessment prior to administering digitalis, and respiratory rate and depth before administering a narcotic. Obtaining an appropriate form of the medication facilitates its administration. A patient may be unable to swallow a tablet and the liquid form of the medication would be effective.

Many pills may be crushed (with exceptions such as enteric-coated, slow-release, and foul-tasting tablets) but determine the crushability of medication before proceeding (phone the pharmacy if unsure). A clean crushing device prevents contamination of the drug with traces of previous drugs.

(This text is adapted and copied from: Tollefson, J. (2012). *Clinical psychomotor skills: Assessment tools for nursing students* (5th ed., p. 137). South Melbourne, Australia: Cengage Learning.

Please answer the following questions

1   How would you reference this in the main body of your writing? Create an **in-text citation**.

_____

(you may need to look at the next chapter for some hints on how to do this, and don't forget to use the page number)

2. Please finish this sentence with a **direct quote** from the text, and use in-text citation.

Clean instruments must be used to crush tablets in order to prevent

_____

_____

_____

3. Please paraphrase by combining sentences 3 and 4 of the paragraph, and use in-text citation.

_____

_____

_____

4. Please summarise the main points of this paragraph, using only one or two sentences, and use in-text citation.

_____

_____

_____

Reference list

A reference list comprises the details of every source cited in a body of work. As it is not logical to include full referencing details within your text, an in-text reference provides the reader with the necessary details (author, date, page number) to locate the source at the end of the work in the reference list. In-text citations in the form of paraphrases, summaries or quotations are supported by the reference list, which details the full referencing details of each source and enables the reader to follow up the cited references for their own purposes.

The format of the reference list will be prescribed in the APA6 referencing guide and topic details.

Regardless of the style, the following referencing details are required by all:

> author(s), organisation or editor(s) responsible for the original work
> year of publication
> title of the work
> title of series and volume number, if applicable
> edition number
> publisher
> place of publication.

The reference system prescribed by the university will list the additional referencing details that are required for specialised sources, including electronic, multimedia, conference papers and newspapers. Chapter 5 will direct you through the techniques for referencing correctly using the author–date referencing guide.

Record all reference details (including page numbers) for each source as you research; this will simplify the task of collating the reference list.

Referencing software

University libraries now provide EndNote referencing software to assist students to manage their references. Your university librarians will provide workshops covering the finer points of using the EndNote software efficiently. Information from the library regarding EndNote can be accessed here http://flinders.libguides.com/endnote.

Whilst the EndNote software is a valuable tool, it does not replace the need to know what, why, when and how to reference. As an active learner, you need to understand the referencing process thoroughly in order to apply it effectively.

You are required to use the American Psychological Association (APA) 6th edition referencing guide at http://www.flinders.edu.au/slc_files/Documents/ Blue%20Guides/APA%20Referencing.pdf.

As you research, it is vital that you develop a system for noting the full reference details (including page numbers) of each source. Make a firm commitment when you take notes to record these details each time you use a new resource, remembering to note the page numbers when you quote or paraphrase. This will enable you to maintain your academic integrity and preserve the intellectual property of others.

EndNote is a referencing software program for storing and managing references. Students of the university may install a copy of EndNote on a single home computer for their own exclusive use. Further information is available from the Library website: http://flinders.libguides.com/c.php?g=735480&p=5255934.

Chapter summary

In academia, it is expected that you will explore, investigate and draw on a range of reference materials and original sources to enrich your understanding of the specific theories, concepts and issues relevant to your particular discipline. When you cite the work of others and collate a reference list, you provide the evidence to support your premise and reinforce your position, whilst also providing the reader with the means to locate the original source. The techniques of in-text citation (quoting, paraphrasing and summarising) provide you with the tools to avoid plagiarism. In-text citations and an accurate reference list supply the means for you to legally acknowledge the original work of others and retain the ethical standards expected in academia.

Summary activities

1. Describe how to make an informed decision about the relevance of a particular source.
2. What is the purpose of referencing every source in your academic work?
3. Why do you draw on the work of others when preparing for an academic assignment?
4. What strategies will you use to maintain your academic integrity?

Reflection

》 How do you benefit from drawing on the work of others through research and writing?
》 What does 'intellectual property' mean for *you* as the author of an original work?

Photo credit

145 © Robert Kneschke/Shutterstock.

5 Use Your Style!
Referencing

Learning Outcomes

By the end of this chapter you will have strategies which enable you to:

> manage references from a range of sources
> apply in-text citations
> use the appropriate techniques to avoid plagiarism
> differentiate between an in-text reference and a reference list entry
> establish academic integrity by acknowledging original sources.

Correct in-text citation and the provision of full referencing details are integral parts of an academic research process and imperative to your success at university. As an active learner, you will use approved citation formats to formally reference and acknowledge the work of others in your academic work. By using the relevant reference style guide, you will be able to incorporate into your writing and presentations a wide range of resources from past and current academic discussions relating to your discipline area.

The referencing style you use permits you to incorporate the ideas of others in your own writing by quoting, paraphrasing and summarising them with accurate citations. In general, an accurate in-text citation will identify the author, year of publication and page number, with full referencing details included. In your research, you will quote, paraphrase or summarise a source written by one or more authors, a source within an edited book or article, or a source within a source.

The sources you choose in your research may be selected from a range of:

- books
- journal articles
- reports
- conference proceedings
- lectures or academic discussions
- professional organisations
- encyclopaedias
- reference materials
- statistics
- standards
- scientific data
- Acts of Parliament
- reviews

Be careful about using these sources

- brochures
- newspaper articles
- radio or TV broadcasts
- podcasts
- vodcasts
- blogs
- social media posts
- personal interviews
- letters
- diaries.

Citation conventions

It is vitally important that you understand the conventions for citing an author's original work to protect their intellectual property. In today's global environment, the resources available are vast and the methods of accessing them are varied; as a result, referencing styles have become complex and sophisticated. It requires an active commitment to learn and practise using referencing styles at university; however, there are definite processes for you to follow which will make the task manageable.

But *how* do I reference properly?

First, check your topic details and get the reference style guide.

TIPS

> Record all reference details as you research and take notes.

> Include the required reference details for in-text citation or footnotes as you write.

> Pay particular attention to the use of punctuation (commas, full stops, colons, brackets, quotation marks) and font style (italics).

> Finally, check and re-check each cited reference within the text and reference list.

Where to locate the referencing details of your chosen source

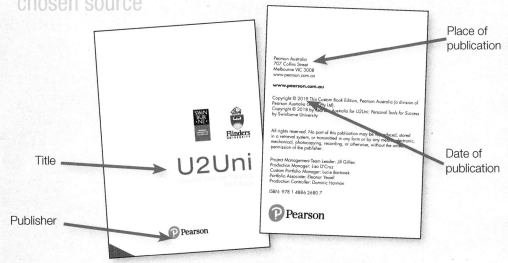

Place of publication

Title

Date of publication

Publisher

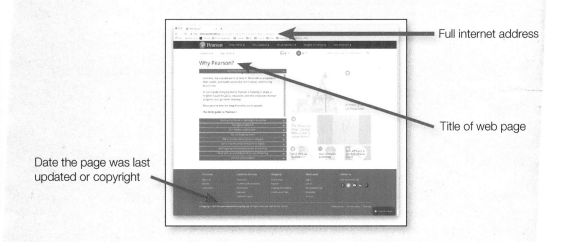

Full internet address

Title of web page

Date the page was last updated or copyright

APA referencing style

There are two components to the APA referencing style: in-text citations and a reference list at the end of the paper which contains full details.

In-text citations

Each time you quote or paraphrase a source or summarise another author's ideas, you must provide an in-text citation. The citation consists of the family name of the author(s), the year of publication and a page number.

The following are two examples of in-text referencing.

> Direct quotation:
> "When we say a person acts 'professionally', for example, we imply that the person is conscientious in actions, knowledgeable in the subject, and responsible to self and others" (Crisp & Taylor, 2009, p. 8).

An ampersand (&) is used in an in-text reference where the authors' names are contained in brackets.

Where two authors of a cited source are incorporated into the text, the word 'and' is used rather than an ampersand (&).

> Paraphrased text:
> Crisp and Taylor (2009, p. 8) define professionals as behaving conscientiously, possessing subject knowledge, and acting responsibly.

In the APA in-text reference style, all direct quotations less than 40 words, are enclosed in double quotation marks. Longer quotations of more than 40 words begin on a new line and are indented (by 1 cm or 5-6 spaces) from the rest of the text. The quoted text font remains the same size as the rest of the text, and one line space is inserted before and after the text. Quotation marks are not required for longer quotations. Text following the longer quotation also begins on a new line.

The basic reference format guide is as follows:

> Author(s) (person, organisation or editor(s)) family name followed by a comma.
> Crisp,

> Author(s) or editor(s) initials – fullstops after initials, one space between the person's initials.
  Crisp, J., & Taylor, C.
> Year of publication in brackets followed by a fullstop.
  Crisp, J., & Taylor, C. (Eds.). (2009).
> Title of the book in italics with minimal capitalisation followed by a fullstop.
  Crisp, J., & Taylor, C. (Eds.). (2009). *Potter & Perry's fundamentals of nursing.*
> Place of publication followed by a colon.
  Crisp, J., & Taylor, C. (Eds.). (2009). *Potter & Perry's fundamentals of nursing* (3rd ed.). Sydney:
> Publisher followed by a full stop.
  Crisp, J., & Taylor, C. (Eds.). (2009). *Potter & Perry's fundamentals of nursing* (3rd ed.). Sydney: Elsevier-Mosby.

Possible additions (if applicable):
> Use an ampersand (&) between two authors' names rather than the word 'and'.
> If more than one author, cite the names in the order in which they appear on the cover page. (Do not rearrange the names alphabetically.)
> An editor (Ed. or Eds.) is acknowledged with the abbreviation.
> If no date is provided – use the abbreviation n.d.
> Sub-title after the title – use minimal capitalisation.
> Title of series and volume number – in italics.
> Include edition number (ed.) – if it is not the first.

Citations within a reference list

Table 5.1 APA style

Information source	Form for in-text reference	Form for reference list or bibliography
BOOKS	Family name, year, page	Author's family name, Initials. (Year). Title. Place of publication: Publisher.
Book with one author	(Tollefson, 2012, p. 108) or Tollefson (2012, p. 108)	Tollefson, J. (2012). *Clinical psychomotor skills: assessment tools for nursing students* (5th ed.). South Melbourne, Australia: Cengage Learning.

Information source	Form for in-text reference	Form for reference list or bibliography
Book with two authors	(Lee & Bishop, 2013, p. 86) or Lee and Bishop (2013, p. 86)	Lee, G. M., & Bishop, P. (2013). *Microbiology and infection control for health professionals* (5th ed.). Frenchs Forest, NSW: Pearson Australia.
Book with three authors	(Harris, Nagy, & Vardaxis, 2009, p. 72) or Harris, Nagy and Vardaxis (2009, p. 72)	Harris, P., Nagy, S., & Vardaxis, N. (2009). *Mosby's dictionary of medicine, nursing and health professions* (2nd Australian and New Zealand ed.). Chatswood, NSW: Elsevier-Mosby.
Book with six or more authors	(Berman et al., 2012) or Berman et al. (2012)	Berman, A., Snyder, S. J., Levett-Jones, T., Dwyer, T., Hales, M., Harvey, N., ... Stanley, D. (Eds.). (2012) *Kozier & Erb's fundamentals of nursing* (2nd Australian ed., Vol. 1). Frenchs Forest, NSW: Pearson Australia.
Book with editor and contributing authors	(Crisp & Taylor, 2013, p. 13) or Crisp and Taylor (2013, p. 13)	Crisp, J., & Taylor, C. (Eds.). (2013). *Potter & Perry's fundamentals of nursing* (4th ed.). Sydney: Elsevier-Mosby.
Chapter in a book	(Bishop, 2013, p. 77) or Bishop (2013, p. 77)	Bishop, P. (2013). Issues in public health. In G. M. Lee & P. Bishop (Eds.). *Microbiology and infection control for health professionals* (5th ed.). Frenchs Forest, NSW: Pearson Australia.
JOURNALS AND PERIODICALS	Author's name, year, page	Author's family name, Initials. (year). Title of article. *Title of Journal, Volume number* (Issue number), page range.
Journal article with single author	(Müller, 2012, p. 130) or Müller (2012, p. 130)	Müller, A. (2012). Research-based design of a medical vocabulary videogame. *International Journal of Pedagogies and Learning, 7*(2), 122–134.

Information source	Form for in-text reference	Form for reference list or bibliography
Journal article with two or three authors	(Hansen & Beaver, 2012, p. 248) or Hansen and Beaver (2012, p. 248)	Hansen, E., & Beaver, S. (2012). Faculty support for ESL nursing students: Action plan for success. *Nursing Education Perspectives, 33*(4), 246–250.
Journal article with four or more authors	(Scheele et al., 2011, p. 246) or Scheele et al. (2011, p. 246)	Scheele, T. H., Pruit, R., Johnson, A., & Xu, Y. (2011). What do we know about educating Asian ESL nursing students? A literature review. *Nursing Education Perspectives, 32*(4), 244–249.
Journal article with author(s) online/electronic journal	(Smith & Pell, 2003, pp. 1459–61) or Smith and Pell (2003, pp. 1459-61)	Smith, G. C. S., & Pell, J. P. (2003). Parachute use to prevent death and major trauma related to gravitational challenge: Systematic review of randomised controlled trials. *BMJ, 327*, 1459-61. Retrieved from http://www.bmj.com/content/327/7429/1459.pdf%2Bhtml
ELECTRONIC RESOURCES	Author's family name, year	Author's family name, Initials. (Year). Title of document or website. Publisher or authoring body where known. Retrieved from (URL).
Online newspaper or magazine article	(Templeman, 2011) or Templeman (2011)	Templeman, S. (2011, May 2). Tertiary education – the policy context. *The Age.* Retrieved from http://www.theage.com.au/
Website	(Gillet, 2014) or Gillet (2014)	Gillet, A. (2014). *Using English for academic purposes.* Retrieved from the UEfAP website http://www.uefap.com/index.htm
Pdf document on a website	(Nursing and Midwifery Board of Australia, 2016) or Nursing and Midwifery Board of Australia (2016)	Nursing and Midwifery Board of Australia. (2016). Registered nurse standards for practice. Retrieved from http://www.nursingmidwiferyboard.gov.au/
A website with no author	(*Hand hygiene,* 2014) or *Hand hygiene* (2014)	*Hand hygiene.* (2014). Retrieved from Hand Hygiene Australia website: http://www.hha.org.au/

Information source	Form for in-text reference	Form for reference list or bibliography
Tables, graphs, diagrams, maps, images on a webpage	(Australian Bureau of Statistics, 2010) or Australian Bureau of Statistics (2010)	Australian Bureau of Statistics. (2010, September quarter). Population growth rate [Graph]. In *Australian Demographic Statistics* (Cat. No. 3103.0). Retrieved from http://www.abs.gov.au/
A government report on a website	(Wake et al., 2002) or Wake et al. (2002)	Wake, M., Harris, C., Hesketh, K., & Wright, M. (2002). *Child health screening and surveillance: A critical review of the evidence*. Retrieved from the National Health and Medical Research Council website: http://www.nhmrc.gov.au/
Pod	(College of Nursing and Health Sciences, 2013) or College of Nursing and Health Sciences (2013)	College of Nursing and Health Sciences. (2013). *Evidence-based practice* [Pod]. Retrieved from http://flo.flinders.edu.au/
CaseWorld™	(College of Nursing and Health Sciences, 2014) or College of Nursing and Health Sciences (2014)	College of Nursing and Health Sciences. (2014). *CaseWorld™ – Greta Balodis* [Case]. Retrieved from http://flo.flinders.edu.au/
From online student learning management system	(Grant, 2012) or Grant (2012)	Grant, J. (2012, March 26). *NURS1103 Health Promotion – Health across the lifespan* [Online lecture]. Retrieved from http://flo.flinders.edu.au/
IMAGES		
Artwork	(Roberts, 1890) or Roberts (1890)	Roberts, T. (1890). *Shearing the rams* [Oil on canvas]. Victoria, Australia: National Gallery of Victoria.

Information source	Form for in-text reference	Form for reference list or bibliography
OTHER		
Personal communication	It has been reported by Kelly personal communication 3 May, 2011 that the topic was discussed.	Cited in text only, not in the reference list, with the person's consent.
From lectures/ tutorials	(J Grant, 2012, lecture, 26 March) Obtain permission from the lecturer/ tutor.	Grant, J. (2012). Lecture 1: Health across the lifespan. Lecture presented for NURS1103, Health Promotion, Flinders University, Bedford Park, South Australia.
Secondary source (source found in a secondary source)	Lasczkowski et al. (cited in Smith & Pell, 2003, p. 1459)	Smith, G. C. S., & Pell, J. P. (2003). Parachute use to prevent death and major trauma related to gravitational challenge: Systematic review of randomised controlled trials. *BMJ, 327*, 1459-61. Retrieved from http://www.bmj.com/. DOI:10.1126/bmj.327.7429.1459

Creating references

Please create reference entries for a book, journal article, and website pdf, as given on this page and overleaf.

CENGAGE
Learning

Clinical Psychomotor Skills: Assessment tools for nursing students
5th Edition
Joanne Tollefson

Publishing manager: Dorothy Chiu
Publishing editor: Fiona Hammond
Developmental editor: Emily Spurr
Project editor: Tanya Simmons
Cover design: Danielle Maccarone and Santiago Villamizar
Text designer: Rina Gargano and Danielle Maccarone
Art direction: Danielle Maccarone
Permissions/Photo researcher: Corrina Tauschke
Editor: Sylvia Marson
Proofreader: Jill Lancashire
Indexer: Julie King
Cover: Corbis; John Smith; Shutterstock.com
Typeset by Cenveo Publisher Services

Any URLs contained in this publication were checked for currency during the production process. Note, however, that the publisher cannot vouch for the ongoing currency of URLs.

For product information and technology assistance,
in Australia call **1300 790 853**;
in New Zealand call **0800 449 725**

For permission to use material from this text or product, please email
aust.permissions@cengage.com

National Library of Australia Cataloguing-in-Publication Data
Tollefson, Joanne.
Clinical psychomotor skills : assessment tools for nursing students / Joanne Tollefson.
5th ed.
9780170216364 (pbk.)
Subjects: Nursing--Practice--Australia.
Nursing--Australia--Ability testing.
Nursing--Standards--Australia.
Clinical competence.
610.730994

Cengage Learning Australia
Level 7, 80 Dorcas Street
South Melbourne, Victoria Australia 3205

Cengage Learning New Zealand
Unit 4B Rosedale Office Park
331 Rosedale Road, Albany, North Shore 0632, NZ

For learning solutions, visit **cengage.com.au**

Printed in China by RR Donnelley Asia Printing Solutions Limited.
2 3 4 5 6 7 16 15 14 13

International Education Journal, 2007, 8(2), 222-236.
ISSN 1443-1475 © 2007 *Shannon Research Press.*
http://iej.com.au

Undergraduate nurse variables that predict academic achievement and clinical competence in nursing

Ian Blackman
School of Nursing and Midwifery, Flinders University *ian.blackman@flinders.edu.au*

Margaret Hall
School of Nursing and Midwifery, Flinders University

I Gusti Ngurah. Darmawan
School of Education, Adelaide University

A hypothetical model was formulated to explore factors that influenced academic and clinical achievement for undergraduate nursing students. Sixteen latent variables were considered including the students' background, gender, type of first language, age, their previous successes with their undergraduate nursing studies and status given for previous studies. The academic and clinical achievement of 179 undergraduate nursing students were estimated by measuring their performance using two separate assessment parameters, their completing grade point average scores and outcomes of their final clinical assessment. Models identifying pathways leading to academic and clinical achievement were tested using Partial Least Square Path Analysis (PLSPATH). The study's results suggest that undergraduate nursing student achievement can be predicted by four variables, which account for 72 per cent of the variance of scores that assess academic and clinical performance at the completion of the third year level of nursing studies. The most significant predictors and those that

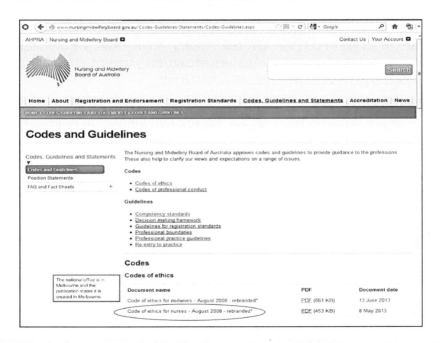

Chapter summary

Referencing is a necessary part of your academic work. It enables you to incorporate the ideas of others into your own work through in-text citation and accurate recording of full referencing details. Referring to your topic details and identifying your discipline's preferred referencing style is essential to ensure you meet these academic requirements. As an active learner, become familiar with and practise using the relevant reference style guide for your discipline area to ensure that you reference precisely and gain confidence in citing. This will enable you to successfully reference to a high academic standard.

Resources

Academic integrity

All students should be familiar with the website 'Academic integrity at Flinders', available from the topic list in FLO. It contains definitions of academic integrity and an explanation of its importance, and tips on how to avoid plagiarism, collusion, or being accused of academic dishonesty. Find out more about the University's policy relating to academic integrity: https://www.flinders.edu.au/content/dam/documents/staff/policies/academic-students/student-academic-integrity-policy.pdf

Referencing

You are required to use the APA referencing guide from the Student Learning Centre: http://www.flinders.edu.au/for_current_students_files/Documents/APA%20Referencing%202018.pdf

EndNote software

EndNote is a database program for storing and managing references. It allows you to import saved references from library catalogues and other electronic databases into EndNote libraries using filters. References in EndNote libraries can be sorted and searched, and incorporated automatically into assignments and papers for publication. Further information is available on the Library website: http://flinders.libguides.com/endnote

Students of the University may install a copy of EndNote on a single home computer for their own exclusive use. To ensure that only people listed under the University site licence can download the software, you will need to log in with your FAN and password at: http://flinders.libguides.com/c.php?g=735408&p=5255934

Reflection

What strategies will you use to ensure that you abide by the conventions of the referencing style guide for your discipline?

What do you understand by the term 'referencing' in an academic environment?

6 Read between the Lines!

Read efficiently

Learning Outcomes

By the end of this chapter you will have strategies which enable you to:

> comprehend highly complex texts

> compare and contrast ideas and information drawn from the text

> select, organise and synthesise information from complex texts

> recognise how features such as register and idiom are used to convey and shape meaning

> interpret, analyse and evaluate texts

> identify audience influence in the writer's choice of text type, structure and language

> reflect on the overt and implied purpose of the text

> apply textual clues to support comprehension

> make use of a broad range of resources to extend understanding.

In day-to-day living we read to acquire knowledge. We need to be able to understand and use this knowledge for a variety of practical applications – for example, reading a shopping list, following instructions, completing medical forms or legal documents and perusing the newspaper. However, reading is *more* than just acquiring knowledge and understanding: it often involves careful analysis and interpretation of text and media for a particular purpose. At university, you will be required to critically analyse as you read. Consequently, it is essential that you develop higher-order thinking skills. This is an active process.

Critical analysis requires you to ask questions, examine, investigate, analyse, compare and contrast, explain, discuss and evaluate different forms of reading materials. These may include business or scientific reports, academic journals or prescribed texts. When you critically analyse, you become actively involved in **assimilating** the information rather than passively accepting it.

Use your dictionary and record any unfamiliar words or terminology.

Dr Benjamin Bloom (1956), an educational academic, developed a mastery learning theory which classified levels of **cognitive** thinking (see Figure 6.1). His approach is useful when illustrating the progression from passively acquiring facts and recalling information, to taking a more active approach: one which involves the complex abilities to analyse, synthesise and evaluate information.

Critical thinking is part of an essential Active Reading Process which involves employing a number of reading strategies to elicit information from complex texts. Developing and practising these reading strategies will empower you to participate fully in the university learning experience.

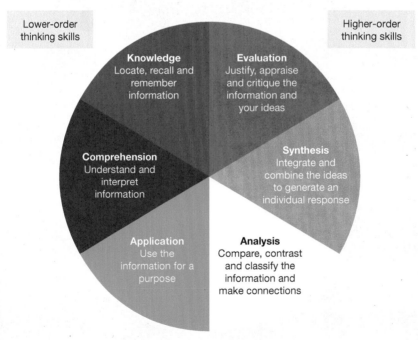

Figure 6.1 A critical analysis model based on Bloom's Taxonomy

If reading is not one of your learning strengths, it is important that you explore ways in which you can interpret reading materials in a way that supports your personal learning style.

Explore your learning style!

Table 6.1 lists some creative reading strategies for different types of learners.

> 'Computers will never take the place of books. You can't stand on a floppy disk to reach a high shelf.' — *Sam Ewing*

Consider how you prefer to learn. What strategies can you think of to develop your ability to critically analyse a text?

Introduction to general reading strategies

Most efficient readers utilise a range of strategies as they read; they do not necessarily read every word. Efficient readers are able to **predict** the reading context using textual clues. These clues enable you to recognise, understand and respond to a text. The following questions are a guide.

> What information does the title of the book, article or journal, or headline of a newspaper tell you about the topic and content?
> Does it provide you with any further information about the writer's contention?
> How does the structure of the text provide a clue to the purpose? For example, how do you find information in a report compared to a table?
> How does the format of the text, including colour, shape, images, numbers and tables, provide extra information?
> How can you use your prior knowledge of words and phrases to clarify meaning?
> How have abbreviations and terminology been used to provide clues about the intended audience, purpose of the text or the sources of evidence?

Table 6.1 Suggested reading strategies

If you prefer to learn through experience and doing, experiment with the following strategies:
> Read part of the text and then write it in your own words.
> If the text has ideas that are interesting, experiment with the ideas and put them into practice.
> Read the text in small chunks: allow yourself a break, walk around, and think or talk about what you have just read before going back to the text.
> Find a good spot to read: you may be uncomfortable at a desk, but lying on the grass outside may be far more enticing.
> Discuss the text with your study group.

If you prefer to learn through seeing and reading, experiment with the following strategies:
> Take particular note of the diagrams, pictures and graphics in the text: carefully examine these and draw meaning from them.
> Use the clues in the layout and structure of the text.
> Use highlighters and colour to draw attention to specific parts of the text.
> Draw diagrams to visually represent the content of the text.
> Write down the key points in diagrammatic form: draw a table or flow chart to create a visual representation of the text.

If you prefer to learn through listening and speaking, experiment with the following strategies:
> Listen to an audio version of the text.
> Use computer software which converts written text to spoken text.
> Record yourself reading the text.
> Read the text out loud.
> Give voice to the text in your head (very useful in the library!).
> Read with others: discuss the content and share ideas.

'I find television very educating. Every time somebody turns on the set, I go into the other room and read a book.' —*Groucho Marx*

The Active Reading Process

What strategies did you use to decipher the text? How challenged were you by this task?

As a student at university, it is vital that you continually develop and refine your active reading skills. To be an effective and efficient reader you need to be actively involved in the reading process and not attempt to absorb the information passively. Passive reading will only allow you to retain a minimal amount of information with limited understanding. This will impact on your ability to effectively utilise the information.

Consequently, as an active reader, you will employ a number of strategies to engage with the text, ensuring you fully understand and can make connections between the text and what you already know. Being an active reader will enable you to successfully paraphrase, summarise and cite from complex texts in your own work.

The Active Reading Process model comprises five stages, as shown in Figure 6.2.

| Pre-read | Skim the text | Scan the text | Read for detail | Critically analyse |

Figure 6.2 Active Reading Process model

1. Pre-read

This is the stage where you familiarise yourself with the *overall aspects* of the text.

Pre-reading provides the 'big picture' view, allowing you to gather broad information about the intention and function of the text, and confirm its potential relevance to your purpose.

> ### 'Big picture' view: identify the key features:
> 1. How is it set out?
> 2. What is the main topic/idea?
> 3. What style of writing is used?
> 4. Is the purpose to inform, instruct, explain or argue?

2. Skim the text

This is the stage where you look for the *key ideas* in the text.

Skim reading the text will give you a broad view of the writer's main point. This will further confirm the relevance of the text.

When you skim read a text, you focus on the surface of the text noting the key words. You are not reading for detail at this stage of the Active Reading Process.

> ### Skim: get an idea of the writer's main points
> › What does the table of contents tell you?
> › What do the headings and/or sub-headings tell you about the content?
> › How do the introduction and conclusion give an overview of the writer's main points?
> › What information do the topic sentences of each paragraph provide?

3. Scan the text

At this stage, you examine (scan) the text to locate the *important information*.

Scanning the text will reveal more specific information which will provide you with the knowledge necessary to proceed to a more in-depth reading.

The writer of a text will often give you hints as to important aspects of the text by using bold, underline, italics, headings, sub-headings: use these hints to help in locating specific information. This will make it easier when you return to the text to read it in more depth.

Use your highlighters and sticky notes to draw attention to the key aspects of the text.

Once you have completed this stage of the reading process, ensure that you write down the main points, relevant ideas and key words.

activity
6.1

Locating information fast

This activity aims to draw your attention to different types of text and encourage you to use reading strategies to find information quickly. These strategies can include looking at headings, skim reading, knowing what kind of information appears in different text types, etc. You should be able to fill in all the gaps within 15 minutes. The readings for this exercise are on the following pages.

This part of the essay discusses immunisation and important factors involving its implementation, focusing specifically on measles and polio. Immunisation is defined as 'a process by which _____ to an infectious disease is induced' (Harris, Nagy & Vardaxis, 2009, p. 876). Immunity is achieved through _____, which is 'any injection of attenuated or _____ microorganisms' (_____, Nagy & Vardaxis, 2009, p. 1795). Often the terms _____ and vaccination are used interchangeably, even though there is some difference in their exact meaning.

In Australia, there is a _____-wide schedule of immunisation (Department of Health, 2013, p. 1). Within this schedule, a single injection is used to immunise against _____, mumps, and rubella (called MMR) and sometimes _____ is included (called MMRV). Australian children first receive an injection for measles when they are _____ old (using the MMR vaccine), and a second injection when they are either _____ old (using the MMRV vaccine) or _____ old (using the _____ vaccine. Similarly, polio vaccinations are given over a set period of time. Vaccinations are given when the child is __ months, 4 months, and __ months old. Immunisation against polio is achieved through the hepB-DTPa-Hib-IPV vaccine, which covers the individual against _____ infectious diseases in total.

Immunisation is not universally accepted around the world. Although immunisation is a routine healthcare activity in many countries, accepted as an effective preventative measure against the severe consequences of common diseases, other countries do not hold the same view. Their decisions can impact not only on their own people, but on other countries around the world, since immunisation works best when whole populations are given vaccines. For example, when the Nigeria government temporarily ceased its _____ vaccination program, the result was a 'resurgences of the importation of polio into _____ countries that had previously been declared free of polio' (Bishop, 2013, p. 339). While Nigeria was the source of the transmission to other _____, the worst affected countries had low herd immunity among their population, since only 52% of their people were immunised against polio. Four countries had long-term _____ of polio. The countries where transmission was controlled had ___% of their population fully immunised (Bishop, 2013, p. ___). When an area has high vaccination coverage, it has a protective effect even for those who are not immunised, or partly immunised, since opportunity for the disease to spread through infected people is reduced greatly.

The perceptions and beliefs of the people about immunisation is important, since these can prevent them from accepting vaccinations. We can again return to Nigeria as an example, this time for _____. Ambe, Omotara and Mandu Baba's (2001, p. 89) study of ___ Nigerian mothers' beliefs about measles found that only 1% perceived immunisation as effective, ___% thought measles immunisation was ineffective, and as much as ___% were unaware of the availability of measles immunisation (Ambe, Omotara & Mandu Baba, 2001, p. 89). Partly, these beliefs about measles immunisation may be related to the mothers' notions about the cause of measles, with 26% attributing this infectious disease to _____ _____ and only 16% identifying an infectious element (Ambe, Omotara & Mandu Baba, 2001, p. 89). It is possible that the attitudes about measles immunisation extend to other types of vaccination, including polio, as discussed in the previous paragraph.

Negative attitudes and beliefs also exist in populations where immunisation has previously been widely accepted. A striking example can be found in the UK. In a small research study involving ___ children, the MMR vaccine was theorised to be an instrumental factor in a chain of events that may ultimately result in _____ (Bishop, 2013, p. 341). While this hypothesised link, and any causality, was thoroughly rejected in large sized _____ studies conducted by _____, many people continued to believe that the MMR vaccine posed an autism risk to their children (Bishop, 2013, p. 341). This resulted in an overall immunisation coverage of 50% in the population, or low herd immunity (Bishop, 2013, p. 341). As a result of low herd immunity and increased infection, measles was reclassified as _____ in the UK, in contrast to the ___-year hiatus of local measles transmission that had previously been achieved (Bishop, 2013, p. 41). Thus, both countries and individuals can greatly affect those who live around them, and this needs to be taken into account in any decision regarding immunisation.

Mosby's dictionary of medicine, nursing and health professions

Harris, P., Nagy, S., & Vardaxis, N. (2009). *Mosby's dictionary of medicine, nursing and health professions* (2nd Australian and New Zealand ed., pp. 876, 1795). Chatswood, NSW: Elsevier-Mosby.

Extract:

immunisation /im´yənīzā´shən/ [L, *immunis*, free from], a process by which resistance to an infectious disease is induced or augmented.

vaccination /vak´sinā´shən/ [L, *vaccinum*, relating to a cow], any injection of attenuated or killed microorganisms, such as bacteria, viruses or rickettsiae, administered to induce immunity or to reduce the effects of associated infectious diseases. Historically, the first vaccinations were administered to immunise against smallpox and used a poxvirus derived from a cow. Vaccinations are now available to immunise against many diseases such as typhoid, measles and mumps. —vaccinate, v.

MMR vaccine and autism

Bishop, P. (2013). Issues in public health. In G. M. Lee & P. Bishop (Eds.). *Microbiology and infection control for health professionals* (5th ed., p. 341). Frenchs Forest, NSW: Pearson Australia.

Extract:

In 1998, a group of British researchers reported the occurrence of an apparently new syndrome of an unusual type of inflammatory bowel disorder (IBD) in a small group of 12 children. The researchers suggested that the measles-mumps-rubella (MMR) vaccine had caused the IBD, when then resulted in decreased absorption of essential vitamins and nutrients through the intestinal tract. They proposed that this could result in developmental disorders such as autism.

Since then, more thorough, large epidemiological studies by WHO have found no evidence of an association. However, many parents in the United Kingdom decided not to vaccinate their children with MMR and the overall coverage rate has fallen to less than 50 per cent. This creates a potential risk for outbreaks of measles and mumps, and the possibility of more cases of congenital rubella. Measles has now been declared endemic again in the UK, 14 years after the local transmission of the measles was halted. The level of coverage is now too low for herd immunity to protect unvaccinated or partially vaccinated people in the community.

National immunisation program schedule

Department of Health. (2013). National immunisation program schedule. Retrieved from http://www.immunise.health.gov.au/internet/immunise/publishing.nsf/Content/08A44BD5B3DD6575CA257BCB00835F83/$File/nip-magnet-v2-2013.pdf

National Immunisation Program Schedule
(As at December 2013)

Immunisation Schedule (0-4 years)

Age	Disease immunised against
Birth	• Hepatitis B *Tick the circles as your child is immunised* ○
2 months can be given at 6 weeks of age	• Hepatitis B, Diphtheria-Tetanus-Whooping Cough, *Haemophilus Influenzae* type b, Polio • Pneumococcal conjugate • Rotavirus ○
4 months	• Hepatitis B, Diphtheria-Tetanus-Whooping Cough, *Haemophilus Influenzae* type b, Polio • Pneumococcal conjugate • Rotavirus ○
6 months	• Hepatitis B, Diphtheria-Tetanus-Whooping Cough, *Haemophilus Influenzae* type b, Polio • Pneumococcal conjugate • Rotavirus** ○
12 months	• *Haemophilus Influenzae* type b, Meningococcal C • Measles, Mumps, Rubella ○
18 months	• Measles, Mumps, Rubella and Varicella (chickenpox) ○
4 years can be given at 3 ½ years of age	• Diphtheria-Tetanus-Whooping Cough and Polio • (Measles, Mumps, Rubella***) ○

Note: Influenza vaccine is available to at risk groups. Additional vaccines are funded for Aboriginal and Torres Strait Islander children in NT, WA, SA and QLD.

** 3rd dose of vaccine dependent on vaccine brand used.
*** to be given only if MMRV vaccine was not given at 18 months.

Perceptions, beliefs and practices of mothers in sub-urban and rural areas towards measles and measles vaccination in Northern Nigeria.

Ambe, J. P., Omotara, B. A., & Mandu Baba, M. (2001). Perceptions, beliefs and practices of mothers in sub-urban and rural areas towards measles and measles vaccination in Northern Nigeria. *Tropical Doctor, 31*(2), 89–90.

Extract:

Context: Measles is of particular concern in Nigeria because of the high fatality rate, and high morbidity rate, particularly in young children. Measles and its complications are a common reason for hospitalization, indicating very low immunization coverage.
Objective: This study was carried out to elucidate the contributing factors from attitudes, beliefs and practices of mothers towards measles and its vaccination.
Design: A cross-sectional survey was conducted in Konduga Local Government Area.
Results: One per cent of the 500 mothers interviewed believed that measles is prevented by immunization, 16% that it is contagious or due to an infectious agent, 26% that it is caused by evil spirits, witchcraft and heat, and 25% had never heard of measles immunization. Twenty-seven per cent said they did not believe immunization was effective and 4% were not allowed to go for immunization by their husbands. Of those mothers whose children had developed measles, only 31% had been treated in formal health facilities. These results indicate an unfavourable attitude and practice by mothers in relation to measles and measles vaccination.
Conclusion: There is the need for an intensive health education campaign to improve this state of affairs and to reduce the morbidity and mortality from measles.

Spotlight on eradication of polio: the importance of herd immunity

Bishop, P. (2013). Issues in public health. In G. M. Lee & P. Bishop (Eds.). *Microbiology and infection control for health professionals* (5th ed., p. 339). Frenchs Forest, NSW: Pearson Australia.

Extract:

However, between 2002 and 2005 there was a resurgence of the importation of polio into 21 countries that had previously been declared free of polio. This was mainly due to the decision by the Nigerian government to suspend its vaccination program, thus reducing the level of herd immunity and allowing the virus to spread to neighbouring countries. Civil unrest in West Africa made the situation worse and the virus spread to the Middle East (carried by pilgrims to the *Haj*). Of the 21 countries affected, four had sustained outbreaks of polio (Indonesia, Somalia, Sudan and Yemen). The countries where transmission occurred had only a 52 per cent rate of vaccination coverage, compared with over 80 per cent in the other countries where transmission of the wild polio virus was able to be controlled. These cases highlight the need to maintain the level of herd immunity in our community.

4. Read for detail

Once you have skimmed and scanned the text, you will need to make a decision about the relevance of this resource and whether to proceed with a more in-depth reading.

To gain a robust understanding of the writer's argument and finally confirm its relevance to your research, you will need to read the text several times, as well as actively take notes.

Read for detail: take notes

> Which reference details need to be added to your reference list?

> What are the writer's key points?

> What supporting evidence does the writer give?

Try to use this strategy for recording information.

Date: _____

Bibliographic details	Key points.	Supporting evidence & annotations.
Include: full bibliographic details	In this section include	→ Note how the main points
Book: title, author, date, publisher details, place of publication.	• the main points	are supported ie. what evidence has the author used to support their argument?
*Note – page number		Include your thoughts & comments in relation to the evidence eg. is the evidence credible or is it based on a tentative assumption?
Journal article : title, author, journal name, volume, date, page numbers & *specific page number you are referring to.		* Add links & make connections to other sources.
Web site : title, author, web address, date viewed.	• Terminology specific to the topic	→ provide an explanation / definition.

5. Critically analyse

This is the final stage of the reading process. It is at this stage that your successful reading strategies will greatly facilitate your capacity to formulate a creative and well-supported argument in an academic format.

There will be many times during your study at university when you will be required to critically analyse a text. After you have skimmed, scanned and read the text thoroughly, you are ready to analyse and evaluate what has been stated, to consider the writer's perspective and to draw your own conclusions.

Having read the text several times, you now need to pause and take the time to think about *what* you have read.

This process will enable you to synthesise the information, to make sense of what you have read, to link new information to what you already know and to ask questions. At this stage it is necessary to consider the information contained in the text from a different angle and read 'between the lines', to gain an overall understanding of the **implicit** meanings concealed within the text. This reading strategy may disclose a perspective which you have not yet considered.

The following critical thinking questions will guide your analysis as you read the text. You will note that some of the questions will ask you to gather knowledge and demonstrate your comprehension of the text. Other questions will require you to think more deeply and consider the implicit meanings in the text.

Critical analysis means you should:

- maintain an objective view;
- determine the key points and examine the evidence;
- read 'between the lines' and look for implicit meanings;
- ask questions;
- consider information from different perspectives;
- identify underlying assumptions;
- evaluate and assess information;
- challenge assumptions;
- investigate alternatives;
- formulate and support your own response.

As a university student you will be required to develop skills in critical analysis. These skills will apply to your reading, note taking, listening to lectures and tutorials, writing for academic purposes, delivering oral presentations and sitting exams. In other words, you need to develop a critical approach to all your learning!

activity 6.2

Explore what is meant by critical thinking. Watch the clip 'What is critical thinking?' before undertaking your own research to further enhance your understanding of this required skill.

<https://www.youtube.com/watch?v=HnJ1bqXUnIM>

Reflect on the following questions as you watch the film clip:

1. What are the skills involved in critical thinking?
2. How might a critical thinker approach a challenge?
3. How does 'black and white thinking' limit your ability to think critically?
4. As a critical thinker, how might you cope with uncertainty?
5. How do the skills of critical thinking empower you as a l earner?

Apply the Critical Thinking Process to all your learning!

activity 6.3

Apply your critical analysis skills to this introductory reading activity. Read the article below and answer the following questions. Keep in mind the five-stage Active Reading Process (see Figure 6.2 on page 185).

1. What do you know about the writer?
2. What is the writer's main contention? List the key points.
3. How does the writer use the evidence to support the contention?
4. How does the writer link the ideas to current opinion and theory?
5. What genre does the writer use to present the argument?
   a. Is it instructional, informative, expository or argumentative, for example?
   b. Does the writer use a particular context to propose the point of view – for example, social, political or religious?
6. Is the evidence valid?
   a. Is the evidence anecdotal or based on authoritative research?
   b. Does the writer make any unsupported generalisations?

7. Does the writer differentiate between fact and opinion?
8. How does the writer demonstrate bias?
9. What persuasive techniques are used to shape meaning?
10. Can you identify how the writer has influenced your viewpoint?
11. How has the writer clarified and/or challenged your own ideas?

Research Note
How does culture reinforce or inhibit critical thinking?

Tiwari, A., Avery, J. A., & Lai, P. (2003). Critical thinking disposition of Hong Kong Chinese and Australian nursing students. *Journal of Advanced Nursing, 44*(3), 298–307.

In a research study conducted in two different countries, Tiwari, Avery and Lai (2003, p. 298) asked the question: How does culture reinforce or inhibit critical thinking?

Cultural differences were identified as significant between Hong Kong undergraduate nursing students and Australian undergraduate nursing students, especially with regards to problem solving in novel situations. While Hong Kong students were just as proficient at problem solving using inductive–deductive reasoning skills in well-known situations, their ability to problem-solve in novel and unprescribed situations was significantly less than the Australian students. How could this be explained? Tests of validity were conducted regarding cultural sensitivity of the instruments prior to conducting the study, including a panel of experts who concluded that the CCTDI (California Critical Thinking Disposition Inventory) being used and translated in Chinese was compatible with local norms and values and the items were designed to measure critical thinking disposition.

Wu (1996) had argued that Chinese people were less inclined to challenge assumptions and question prescribed views for fear of being disrespectful to their elders or senior people. Dardess (1999) argued that a strong cultural norm of not revealing one's feelings or thoughts (called *bugou yanxiao*) in Chinese communities inhibits a critical thinking culture.

Critical analysis is a complex skill, which requires both lower- and higher-order thinking skills. A thorough understanding of these is necessary in order for you to progress from simply acquiring facts and recalling information, to actively analysing, synthesising and evaluating information. The Critical Analysis Reading Rubric (see Table 6.2) is a valuable tool for appraising your ability to critically analyse. As an active learner, gathering and assessing this information about your skill level can inspire you to reach the highest standard of critical thinking.

Table 6.2 Critical Analysis Reading Rubric

Cognitive thinking skill	Developing	Progressing	Strengthening
	Knowledge Comprehension	Application Analysis	Synthesis Evaluation
Determine key points	I identified: > the writer's key points using the heading, topic sentences and the structure of the text.	I interpreted: > key points and examined the key words and terminology after skimming and scanning the text; > the main argument by looking in detail at the structure of the text and how the paragraphs link.	I evaluated: > the writer's sequence of ideas to determine the main argument; > the link between the writer's ideas; > the relevance of the ideas by examining the writer's rationale.
Examine the evidence	I located: > the evidence used by the writer, including graphs, diagrams, tables; > the source of the evidence; > how the evidence supported the contention.	I examined: > the style of evidence used by the writer – for example, anecdotal, expert opinion or statistical; > the facts and opinions; > aspects of the evidence which did not support the main argument.	I assessed: > the currency, validity, relevance and sufficiency of the evidence; > the way the writer represented the views of others; > effectiveness of how the evidence was incorporated.
Interpret implicit meaning	I recognised: > the writer; > the source.	I questioned: > the writer's knowledge; > how this influenced the text.	I considered: > the influences on the writer's point of view, by researching further; > issues which may have been excluded, intentionally or unintentionally.

continues

Table 6.2 Critical Analysis Reading Rubric *continued*

	Developing	Progressing	Strengthening
Explore the argument	I explained: 〉 the writer's argument (and any opposing argument) by paraphrasing.	I analysed: 〉 the arguments presented; 〉 how the writer expressed different perspectives; 〉 the choice of words and phrases to convey meaning; 〉 the sequence and structure of ideas.	I appraised: 〉 the connections between the stated argument and the implicit meaning; 〉 ideas taken out of context, and underlying assumptions or bias; 〉 the application of theory to the argument; 〉 the use of persuasive techniques.
Formulate own response	I expressed: 〉 how I agreed/disagreed with the writer's argument and supported my conclusions with information from the text.	I created: 〉 a list of questions to clarify information; 〉 a response to the text by connecting prior knowledge with the new information.	I composed: 〉 a list of references which gave me greater insight into the text; 〉 a response by **critiquing** new information and comparing it to current knowledge and theory; 〉 an argument, and drew conclusions using supporting evidence from the text and other relevant sources.

Chapter summary

Reading is *more* than just acquiring knowledge and understanding. It is an *active* process which involves the complex abilities of analysis, synthesis and evaluation.

In any discipline at university you will be required to read and critically analyse texts. Consequently, it is essential that you develop higher-order thinking skills. As you apply the Active Reading Process model to the critical analysis of text, you will become a more proficient reader who can assimilate information, rather than passively accept it. This will empower you to participate fully in the university learning experience.

Summary activity

What steps will you use to critically analyse a text?

Reflection

Now consider how you will apply what you have learned.

» What changes do you need to implement in your study routine to accommodate your strengths and challenges?
» How will you put these changes into practice?
» How will these changes impact your learning at university?

Photo credit

181 © Monkey Business Images/Shutterstock.

7 Stress Less!
Survive examinations

Learning Outcomes

By the end of this chapter you will have strategies which enable you to:

> design, manage and monitor your learning for examinations
> apply your prior skills and knowledge to a new context
> actively engage in learning
> set goals
> identify your personal learning strengths and areas of challenge
> revise, recall, and reflect on learning
> select and implement active learning strategies.

At university, you are required to demonstrate your understanding of a topic by applying it to a range of assessments: by writing assignments (including essays, reports, case studies), making oral presentations, participating in tutorial activities, completing online assessments, or sitting for examinations. Each of these methods of assessment provides you with an opportunity to prove that you understand and can apply your topic knowledge to a question, a hypothesis or a problem to solve. Examinations are one method employed by lecturers to determine your level of comprehension, how well read you are in your discipline and how proficiently you apply your learning. This is much more than simply requiring you to regurgitate facts, and requires a serious and analytical approach to study.

Preparing for exams can be stressful, but by taking responsibility for your own learning and revision, and implementing an Active Learning Approach (Chapter 1), new knowledge is more confidently processed, reviewed, recalled and applied. If you have practised this approach from the beginning, you will be better prepared, organised and less anxious at exam time!

> 'Learning isn't about being smart enough; it is about being motivated enough.' —*M. Ferguson*

The purpose of examinations

The main purpose of examinations is to determine how well you know your discipline area. From the responses you give, examiners will be able to determine how much of the topic content you have absorbed. They will be able to identify if you have a substantial grasp of the facts and theories provided in lectures and tutorials, and whether you have not only read the prescribed reading, but also researched further. However, this is not the sole purpose of exams. Examiners also want to ascertain how effectively you can apply the new knowledge to situations or problems, and how proficiently you can analyse and evaluate this knowledge to formulate and support a position. Your ability to do this effectively under exam conditions will require your adherence to an Active Learning Approach and thorough exam preparation.

Preparing for exam time

Maintain a healthy balance between study and life

Employing an Active Learning Approach to your study is an excellent exam preparation method. It will provide you with effective strategies to manage your revision and enable you to be successful in your examinations. Here are a few important tips to keep in mind as you prepare:

> Maintain a regular sleep routine.

To minimise stress and keep healthy, ensure that you:
- Sleep no less than eight hours per night
- Keep a regular bedtime during the week
- Switch off your mobile phone when you go to bed.

> Eat well.

To maintain your energy levels, provide 'food for your brain', which will help you concentrate more effectively and stay healthy:

- Eat foods which are high in protein and low in carbohydrate, and include plenty of fruit and vegetables.
- Enjoy three main meals a day, plus two snacks. (Remember: you may eat as much fruit and vegetables as you like!)
- Drink plenty of water – at least two litres a day. (Refrain from caffeinated drinks.)

> Make time to relax.

Re-energising through taking time to relax is not negative time away from study but a productive means to re-group. Step away from the intensity of your study and return feeling refreshed and more effective:
- Do something you enjoy or which makes you laugh! (This will encourage endorphins, which help to reduce stress levels.)

'Laughter is inner jogging.' —*Norman Cousins*

> Maintain a positive attitude.

To keep you focused and motivated:
- Write affirmations: Stay strong! Keep calm! You are doing well! ☺
- Use positive self-talk as a source of encouragement.

> Set realistic and achievable goals for study.

Develop a practical exam revision routine to minimise stress!

> Prioritise your most important tasks and commitments.

To minimise your anxiety and maintain a manageable routine:
- List the things you like doing, and do something from this list to reward yourself.

> Create a comfortable study space.

To achieve the maximum benefit out of the time you allocate to exam revision:
- Ensure that your study area is set up ergonomically with adequate lighting and ventilation.

> Plan ahead.

To reduce the pressure of exam time:
- Organise your time well in advance
- Begin revision from week one and consolidate your learning continually, as well as in the weeks leading up to the exams.

> Establish a support network.

To minimise nervous tension around exam time:
- Advise family and friends
- Revise with your study group.

Enjoy accessing social networking sites as a reward *after* a study session.

What preparation do I need to do?

Revising for an exam requires preparation and prudent planning. An active learner will be confident in this process. Attendance at all the lectures and tutorials throughout the semester, and completion of all the set readings and assignments, is a small part of exam revision. As an active learner you will take a proactive approach to your exam preparation by attending final lectures and tutorials, and by finding out as much as you can about the content and type of examination.

Set realistic goals

Setting realistic goals at the beginning of the semester – and continually reviewing them – is a valuable strategy for minimising stress at exam time. If you have set realistic and achievable goals from the beginning, you will be more successful at managing your workload and staying stress free. Prior to exam time, review these goals and make a list of your short-term goals for the examination period. (Presumably, your long-term goal will be to have success in your exams!) This process will help you maintain focus, minimise your anxiety levels and assist you to create a manageable study schedule. When reviewing your goals before examination time, consider the points set out in Figure 7.1.

> Be flexible and kind to yourself – do not worry about things that happen in life over which you have no control, such as getting a cold!
>
> Be proactive instead of reactive, and respond accordingly. Do what you CAN manage; refocus your goals and get support.

Create a realistic revision schedule

After you have reviewed and reorganised your exam goals, you can create a study plan around your goals (see Figure 7.2). As an active learner, you will have been revising since the first week: making topic summaries; clarifying any questions or uncertainties as you go; and reading widely to extend your knowledge and understanding. This will ensure that the new learning transfers from your short-term memory into your long-term memory, for more effective recall at examination time. The time directly prior to exams is when you need to be consolidating your knowledge and applying it to different scenarios.

1. Decide exactly what you hope to achieve in a day:
   - *How long* you will spend on revision.

     In the morning before work, or after dinner?
   - *What* you will revise.

     Lecture notes, chapter summaries, each topic, past exam papers?
   - *When* you will schedule time for exercise. (Aim for 30 minutes a day.)

     Twice a week for team sport, or a swim/walk/jog every other day?
2. Determine the minimum you need to do to achieve your goals.

   An hour every day per topic?
3. Ensure your goals are achievable.

   Do not push yourself to the limit trying to achieve the impossible – such as studying every hour of the day. This may lead to burn-out.
4. Make certain that your goals can be reached within a manageable timeframe.

   If you still need to work whilst studying for exams, make certain that you can cope with the added pressure.
5. Prioritise what you MUST do.

   Reschedule less pressing tasks until after the exams.
6. Draw up a revision timetable.

   Use colour to highlight areas of most importance.
7. Allocate specific revision times with your study group.
8. Plan times away from study to relax and wind down.

Figure 7.1 Prioritising goals at exam time

Identify the exam period, then create your own revision schedule (having already established your goals). Use the following suggestions to guide your planning:
1. Decide how much time you will allocate to revision.
2. Consider the material you need to revise.
3. Determine whether you have been given any parameters by your lecturers.
4. Record the date of each exam and plan your study times accordingly.
5. Establish how much time you need to allocate to revising each unit.
6. Ensure your revision time is well spent.
7. Allow time for breaks and avoid getting bogged down.
8. Record relaxation or reward time in your schedule.

Sample exam revision plan: Semester one 2011

Semester one	2 May	9 May	16 May	23 May	30 May	6 June	13 June
Unit	9	10	11	12	13	14	15
Unit A	Make & review chapter summaries		Class oral presentation	Revise summaries ture/lecture notes.	Exam revision week / Practise exam.	Oral exam / Exam Period	Written exam / Exam Period
Unit B	Re-read text book - Chapters 1-6 & make summaries		Term paper due	Review all notes & practise writing essay	Practise exam revision week in time limit / Exam revision week	Exam Period	Exam / Exam Period
Unit C	Listen to lecture podcasts and review tutorial notes.	Multiple choice Quiz	Term paper due	Revision Quiz-class / Ask Q if unsure	Practise short answer Q / Exam revision week	Exam / Exam Period	Exam Period
Unit B	Read over lecture & ture notes. / Term paper due		Study group - revision	Revision Quiz-class	Practise multiple choice & essay writing. / Exam revision week	Exam / Exam Period	Exam Period

Finished!
Celebrate!

Figure 7.2 Sample revision plan

Actively revise!

> Make summaries as you go and actively engage with your notes.

> Write your notes in longhand to practise your handwriting skills. In exams you will have to write by hand, so it is very important to ensure that your writing is legible. Anything an examiner cannot read will lose marks.

> Determine the best time of day for you to study – when you are most alert and able to concentrate.

> Revise your summaries a few days later – highlight the key points.

> Read your notes aloud to reinforce what you remember.

Beginning your revision

If you have followed an Active Learning Process throughout the semester, you will be ahead when you come to begin your exam revision. As you begin, consider the purpose of exams. An exam will:

> determine how well you know your topic area

> identify that you have a substantial grasp of facts and theories provided in lectures

> establish whether you have read wider than the prescribed readings

> ascertain how effectively you can apply the new knowledge to situations or problems

> determine how proficiently you can analyse and evaluate knowledge, and formulate and support a position.

You will need to be certain that your exam preparation and revision covers each of these purposes. Identifying what you already know and understand about the topic will assist you in knowing what you need to research further and what you will need to recall. It is essential that you allow time to practise your recall and application of information under exam conditions. This is important so that you can identify areas which may impede your success during the examination. By setting a time limit for a response, for instance, you can ascertain whether you are able to complete a valid response in the given time. Additionally, you may find (or know) that your nerves limit your ability to recall relevant information; thus, practising under exam conditions, prior to the actual exam, will provide you with the opportunity to establish strategies to manage these issues. Above all, be active in your approach to exam preparation. The following strategies may be useful to get you started.

Exam revision strategies

1. Use active note-taking skills

   Check your topic details to establish that you have adequate notes on every aspect of your topic. Print out the overview of the materials covered, and highlight those which require your attention.

If you need to print a document, use both sides of the sheet of paper.

Highlight your lecture notes and make topic summaries using your own words.

Develop a glossary of key words and terminology you need to know.

Construct a concept map of the main ideas, facts and theories you have collated on each topic – from lectures, tutorials, readings and discussions.

Format your own visual cues or pictures, and reconstruct your notes into lists, charts and diagrams to aid your recall.

Use your textbook summaries and any activities or questions to practise and apply your learning.

Write responses to past exam questions to test your understanding of the knowledge learned.

Check your answers and follow up on any gaps in your knowledge.

Challenge yourself with solving problems using the facts and theories you have studied.

Cover sections of a text or your notes and test whether you can recall the relevant information.

Check the prescribed reading lists and read any texts you have missed to improve your topic knowledge – taking note of the main points.

2. Use active learning strategies

Make meaningful connections between facts, theories and ideas as you revise. (A concept map will help you here.)

Apply the information to real-life situations to give it purpose.

Employ memory strategies, such as repetition, rhymes, songs, acronyms and mnemonics, to help you recall information, terminology and discipline-specific vocabulary.

Explain your knowledge to someone outside of your topic area. This will reinforce what you know well and what you may need to revise further.

Clarify any questions you have with your lecturer or tutor.

Revise with your study group – debate what you know to consolidate your understanding, and brainstorm problems.

3. Apply critical thinking strategies as you practise past examination papers – for example

What do the directive verbs tell you about the parameters of the task?

What points might you make in an argument?

What evidence can you recall to validate your position?

How would you structure and develop a contrary point of view?

What causes and effects are relevant?

How can the question or topic be applied to theory?

What problems are involved, and how might they be solved?

Using active learning, note taking and critical thinking strategies in your exam revision will improve your understanding and application of the subject matter and strengthen your ability to respond effectively in exams.

Study creatively. Establish active learning strategies to improve your knowledge and understanding. Don't just memorise chunks of information.

'To solve any problem, here are three questions to ask yourself: First, what could I do? Second, what could I read? And third, who could I ask?' —*Jim Rohn*

Types of exams

The type of examination will be dependent on your discipline area. Regardless of the type of examination, it is vital that you prepare and practise as often as possible during the exam preparation period. Completing past exams or sample questions within the required time limit will improve your confidence, deepen your understanding, and equip you with strategies for approaching exam questions when you sit the actual examination. Ensure that you practise a variety of question types so that you will not be caught by surprise in the examination.

Formal referencing is generally not required in exams. Check the exam guidelines in your topic details for details.

Essays

Essays in exams are designed to test your understanding and application of new learning by giving you the opportunity to:

> demonstrate that you can analyse, discuss, debate, compare and contrast effectively using the essay structure
> express ideas clearly and logically
> display knowledge of important issues, concepts and theories relevant to the topic

> provide a succinct response to the essay question in the form of a reasoned and well-organised argument, validated by evidence
> select appropriate academic language
> employ correct spelling and grammar.

In the exam, you will need to employ your critical thinking skills to analyse the question or topic given – that is, you will be required to identify the instruction verbs, key words and terminology before constructing a concept map and making a plan. You will significantly improve your chances of success in an exam if you make use of an Active Learning Approach during the pre-exam weeks. This time provides you with the opportunity to hone your essay writing skills by practising sample essay questions within a time constraint. The more you practise, the more proficient you will become at analysing a question, constructing a concept map and plan, and crafting a well-organised and logical piece of academic writing.

Developing a plan before you begin writing is time well spent. It not only provides you with a sound structure, but will also enable the examiner to review your ideas and thinking around the topic in the unfortunate event that you have been unable to finish within the allocated time. It is possible that you may be allocated some marks for your planning, if this indicates clarity of thought and content. Consequently, ensure that your plan clearly:

> identifies the position you will take
> indicates the topic for each paragraph
> notes the theories, examples or evidence to which you will refer.

Referring to your plan as you write your exam essay will assist you in expressing your thoughts clearly and succinctly, and will prevent you from wandering off on a tangent. When you have finished writing, review your essay or leave plenty of time at the end of the exam to consider whether you have:

> addressed every aspect of the question
> made a clear plan for the examiner to identify
> related your main ideas to the topic or question asked
> incorporated relevant theories and valid evidence

> applied your critical thinking skills to the topic by making comparisons, evaluations or interpretations of theories, others' perspectives or evidence
> strictly followed the essay writing structures
> crafted a strong introduction which clearly identifies the position you will take (including key words and terminology and any limitations)
> constructed logical sentences and paragraphs supported with evidence
> developed your main points with precision, identifying connections between each paragraph
> used appropriate and grammatically correct academic language and clear connective words and phrases
> avoided repetition.

Your ability to write an effective essay under exam conditions will depend largely on your consistent study and preparation from the beginning. Reading widely and systematically will prepare you to competently draw on your acquired knowledge and understanding, make comparisons between researchers, theories and perspectives, and identify relationships, connections and counter-arguments to the question posed. Examiners will look closely to establish evidence of your wider reading, which will be apparent in the evidence and supporting arguments you provide.

When writing an essay or giving short answers under exam conditions, remember the following strategies:

> Incorporate the wording of the question into your introduction or first sentence.
> Use the key words and terminology throughout your response to keep you focused on the topic.
> Use clear transition and connective words to allow you to segue smoothly, organise your ideas and provide a guide to the examiner.
> Provide the examiner with an unambiguous guide as to the direction of your argument or response in your introductory sentence or paragraph.

This tip is relevant for all exams.

Always ensure that your handwriting is legible in exam responses. If your writing cannot be interpreted by the examiner, it may not be considered at all.

Short answers

Examiners sometimes prefer short answer questions which give you the opportunity to express what you know in your own words. The length of your response will depend on the instruction given or the complexity of the question itself. The number of marks allocated to the question will also indicate how many points you are required to make. Basically, short answer questions aim to:

> assess your knowledge of the content of the topic
> test your critical thinking skills
> determine how concisely, accurately and clearly you can express a response.

In the exam, ensure that you analyse the question carefully before responding. It is essential that you fully understand the instruction verbs and key words, before checking for any limiting words or phrases which may provide the parameters for your response. In a short answer response, you may need to consider any assumptions made in the topic question. This is when your ability to think critically will greatly support your learning. Before you respond, briefly brainstorm your ideas around the question, keeping in mind that you will need to cover all aspects of the topic. Check the marks allocated to the question to determine how much detail the examiner might expect and ensure that you answer the question within the allocated time. You must always answer in full, grammatically correct sentences, with correct spelling, in accordance with academic standards.

Multiple choice

Multiple choice questions require a thorough knowledge base and sound critical thinking skills to do well. They are often chosen by examiners to test your knowledge by distracting you with false answers or answers which are close to the truth, but not quite. This can be quite daunting if you are not familiar with this format. Practising how to answer multiple choice questions will allow you to become confident in your subject matter, as you learn how to carefully read, dissect and analyse the questions and/or instructions in order to provide the correct response. Generally, multiple choice examinations are intended to:

> test your memory for detail
> assess your ability to discriminate between details in the possible answers.

'One must learn by doing the thing. For though you think you know it, you have no certainty until you try.' —*Sophocles*

When you complete practice exams as part of your revision plan, you will become aware that there are several types of multiple choice questions. You will need to rely on both your knowledge and understanding of the topic, as well as your critical thinking skills, when selecting correct responses to any of these question types. A few of these include:

> **True/False questions:** These questions require you to select either the 'true' (correct) or the 'false' (incorrect) answer. Do not be fooled into thinking that these are easy questions. Frequently, false answers (which may only indicate very subtle differences) are included to distract you from the true answer.

> **Odd one out:** These questions require you to identify a pattern amongst the alternatives and then choose which option is the 'odd one out'.

> **Most accurate:** These questions ask you to select the 'most accurate' answer, and will require a careful analysis and consideration to determine the correct answer. Be mindful, as they are designed to confuse you.

> **Extension questions:** As the name infers, these questions will provide you with part of a sentence which you are required to accurately complete.

Overall, multiple choice exams are usually carefully designed to minimise the 'luck' factor and require you to know your material extremely well. However, if you are not sure about an answer, have a reasonable guess, put a mark beside that question, and keep going. At the end of the exam you may have sufficient time to revisit the questions you have marked and double-check your answers.

Problem-solving questions

Problem-solving questions require you to use a range of critical thinking skills. They are frequently preferred across a number of discipline areas because they focus not only on the acquisition and retention of knowledge, but also on its evaluation and application to a variety of real situations. In an examination, problem-solving questions are used to:

> test your ability to describe, identify and analyse information or scenarios

> determine your ability to question and evaluate problems, define the issues and generate possible solutions

> accurately apply appropriate solutions or methods to a range of scenarios or challenges.

To be successful in your responses you will need to ensure that you have a comprehensive understanding of the theoretical principles and formulae which underpin a classification of a problem or scenario. Using past exams and sample questions in your planning and preparation will enable you to practise these skills and applications. Examiners will allocate marks based on your ability to apply the relevant theory or formula to the given scenario, case study or problem. An examiner will also register the process you have taken to reach a successful or appropriate outcome.

Problem solving often involves common key elements. Consider the following questions as you respond to a problem:

> What information has been supplied?
> How does this relate to what you already know?
> What else might you need to consider?
> What can you determine about the type of problem from the information supplied?
> What theory or formula is applicable?

The techniques you would employ in your approach to any examination are applicable to exams involving problem-solving questions. In this type of exam, you will rely heavily on a high standard of critical thinking skills. By taking an Active Learning Approach to all your studies, you will ensure that you develop those skills.

When you begin the exam, take the time to write notes next to each of the problems you intend to answer before responding in full. This is not dissimilar to a brainstorming technique. Using the questions above will help you to identify the type of problem and how to formulate a response. Your notes are a guide for you, and may also provide the examiner with a little information about how you might have responded in the event you are unable to complete the question.

In each response it is essential that you clearly identify the approach you have taken, the steps made to reach your solution, and the theoretical principles or formula rules you have applied. Identify these when you review your response and ensure that you have correctly responded to all parts of the question.

Ensure you plan your time well and leave an adequate amount of time to review and edit your answers at the end of the exam.

Open book

Open book examinations generally permit you to take a prescribed textbook or two pages of notes into the exam. Whilst this might seem like a gift, do not be fooled! You will still be required to prepare thoroughly for this type of exam, as you would for any other type. An open book examination will aim to:

> identify how well you know your topic content
> test how efficiently you can locate and use the relevant information in your textbook
> examine how you apply the information contained in your notes.

In an open book exam you will apply the techniques which are pertinent to all the other types of exams. You will need to have a thorough understanding of your subject matter, in addition to being completely familiar with your textbook. Ensure that you can identify and refer to any part of the text (including the contents and index pages) so that you can efficiently identify the correct place in the book under exam conditions.

Whilst preparing for an open book exam, it is often useful to construct concept maps or make summaries of relevant chapters or your notes (from lectures, tutorials and readings) to facilitate your familiarity with the subject matter. This will enable you to use your own words to avoid plagiarism in exam conditions. It is essential that you know *exactly* where to find what you need, rather than waste valuable writing time searching. Active learners will be well supported by their thorough preparation and consistent approach to study from the beginning and will be able to rely on their accumulated knowledge.

Online tests

Online tests are usually formative, but may be summative, assessments used to gauge your level of understanding on a specific topic, before proceeding to the next topic in the course. Online quizzes or interactive activities aim to test your knowledge and understanding. They are carefully monitored and are usually timed. An online quiz or activity can contain a variety of question types, including true/false, multiple choice, match the answer and fill in the blanks; these provide you with immediate feedback and, as such, are an effective self-assessment tool.

How will you approach your exam preparation?

Active learners prepare well!

Seek support

There are times when you may feel that you need the help of others to gain perspective and develop strategies to manage. Sometimes the pressure of exams can be overwhelming and you may need reassurance from a friend, a study group member, tutor, or support service. You may require help to develop an exam revision schedule, which a learning skills advisor would provide; alternatively, you may wish to speak to a student counsellor to share your concerns. It is much better to seek this support when you first realise the need, rather than let it continue to stress you and develop into something beyond your control. Persevere until you find the right help to meet your needs. The first person you go to may not always be the most appropriate.

Acknowledging that you need help is a strength, not a weakness.

There may be times when special circumstances may affect your results, such as a prolonged illness, a form of hardship or some other trauma. In any of these situations, you can apply for special consideration. Check university protocols to understand the special consideration process in the event you may need to apply.

It is generally required that an application for special consideration is lodged a few days prior to an exam and is substantiated with a medical certificate if relevant. However, there are emergency circumstances where this is not possible, and you will need to contact the college office for advice.

The exam

The day before the exam

Think positively! Active learners prepare well and will have accumulated knowledge into their long-term memory. If this is you, congratulate yourself; you are well prepared for the exam!

In contrast, cramming at the last minute is *not* effective; you will not have a thorough understanding of the information or be able to apply it. What *is* useful the night before the examination is to do the following:

> Read over your summary notes.
> Talk about what you know.
> Review the text for your open book exam.
> Confirm the location of the examination.
> Double-check FLO for last-minute exam announcements.
> If driving, check the fuel gauge.
> Consider a transport contingency plan.
> Prepare the equipment you need:
> - a range of pens, pencils, rubber, highlighter
> - bottle of water (if permitted)
> - open book exam materials
> - student identification
> - calculator
> - wrist watch.
> Relax:
> - Watch a favourite TV program.
> - Go online.
> - Play sport.
> - Have coffee with a friend.
> Maintain your regular sleep pattern.
> Set an alarm so that you have plenty of time.

It is very normal to feel anxious about an exam, even *with* thorough preparation. It is a natural human response to a stressful situation, where the hormone adrenalin triggers an increase in your blood circulation and breathing. You may become aware of signs which are symptomatic of this; however, remember that each individual reacts differently. These symptoms may include:

> accelerated heart rate
> insomnia
> shallow breathing
> nausea
> 'butterflies' in the stomach
> headache
> dry mouth.

At the time, these symptoms may seem concerning and may impact your ability to recall information. Having an awareness of this normal process will enable you to manage the symptoms.

> Relax by doing something you enjoy, either alone or with others.
> Breathe deeply.
> Meditate.
> Do stretching exercises.
> Listen to music.

Above all, stay calm in the knowledge that you have prepared well.

The day of the exam

When deciding what to wear, take into consideration the exam environment. Confirm that you have your exam equipment and, regardless of whether the exam is in the morning or the afternoon, ensure that you are hydrated and have eaten a balanced meal. Plan for unexpected circumstances and arrive at the exam venue before the prescribed time.

During the exam

Remain calm and focused. Talk positively to yourself, staying confident in the knowledge that you have prepared well, and do the best you can. The exam will be monitored by at least one member of academic staff, sometimes known as an invigilator. When you enter the examination venue, find your seat, arrange your equipment, locate the clock, turn

off your mobile phone, take three deep breaths and await instructions from the invigilator! Take particular note of any administrative requirements and emergency instructions.

Reading time

Each exam will have reading time of approximately 10–15 minutes. This is valuable reading time; therefore, use it effectively to familiarise yourself with the overall content and structure of the exam. It is also imperative, during the reading time, to read the examination cover sheet carefully for all the specific procedural instructions to candidates.

The examination cover sheet (see Figure 7.3) will confirm the total percentage of marks allocated and establish parts contained within the exam. On continuing your reading you will identify the following:

> the composition of each part
> the type of exam questions
> the allocated marks for each question
> the instructions and expectations for each question
> the compulsory questions
> the elective questions
> the questions which provide you with a choice.

Ensure that you read each page, including the back cover, before returning to the beginning to reread and select your questions/topics based on your knowledge. At this stage it is prudent to prioritise the order in which you will respond to questions; this will be dependent on:

> your knowledge base
> your skill strengths
> the allocation of marks to the task

Last Name	First Name	Student ID No.	Desk No.

Semester 1 2013 Examinations

Topic No/s: NURS 2724

Topic Name/s: Indigenous Health For Nurses

Reading Time: 15 mins
Examination Duration: 2 hours
Pages (including cover): 8
Questions: Students must answer 14 of the 17 questions

Instructions to Candidates

Open Book Exam : 1 of the two core texts is allowed

Section 1. 10 Multiple Choice Questions	**2 marks each = 20**
Section 2. Choose 3 of the 5 Short Answer questions	**10 marks each= 30**
Section 3. Choose one of two Short Essay questions	**50 marks = 50**

Calculators

Calculators not required

Materials Permitted

One of the following texts

1.Taylor and Guerin 2010 Health Care and Indigenous Australians

2. Eckermann et al 2010 Binan Goonj : Bridging Cultures in Aboriginal Health

Students may also use 1 A4 sheet of notes printed on one side

Materials Required

Writing pens

Students must hand in this paper at the end of the examination

DO NOT TURN OVER PAPER UNTIL PERMITTED

Figure 7.3 Examination cover sheet

> your comfort zone
> the type of exam.

Prioritising the order will be totally subjective and will vary for each individual. However, it is wise to approach the questions allocated the majority of marks while you are still fresh. The next stage is to estimate the amount of time you will need to allocate to each question with regard to the total exam time. Always allow a percentage of the total time to review your answers (for example, 10–15 minutes for an exam lasting 2½ to 3 hours).

Stay focused, and maintain your own personal zone to avoid being distracted by others.

Writing time

The invigilator will indicate when you are permitted to begin writing and you must not pick up a pen prior to this. Having analysed the contents of the exam in your reading time, you will be able to note down your immediate thoughts beside the questions you have selected, which will act as a prompt when you return to write. Record the amount of time you have decided to allocate to each question. Write out any mnemonics, acronyms, formulae, data or figures that specifically relate to a question. Having established the order in which you will respond, you can now begin to look at individual questions. Reread and analyse the question, and employ your critical thinking skills to construct a response. Remember to write legibly and make notes or plans wherever possible.

We all suffer from blank memories every now and then; nevertheless, this is quite common under the pressure of exams. There are a number of strategies which you might try to get you going!

1. Relax! Focus on slowing down your breathing. Shut your eyes for a few minutes and listen to your breathing.
2. Reread the question – ensure that you have interpreted it correctly, understood the key words and not overlooked any information.
3. Brainstorm the question – begin by writing the topic on a piece of paper and focus on the key words to trigger other thoughts. However, do not spend too long on this if nothing comes to mind; come back to it later.
4. Take a calculated guess at the answer – this is relevant to multiple choice questions, but it should only be used as a last resort. If you take a guess, use your critical thinking skills to limit the options.

'It's not too late at all. You just don't yet know what you are capable of.' —*Mahatma Gandhi*

Strategies for maximising your exam marks

> Attempt every question, even if you only jot down a brief response.
> If you are not sure of the answer, paraphrase the question and explore connections and links.
> Watch your time and stay focused, and avoid spending too long on difficult questions.
> Answer the compulsory questions first.
> Make sure your response is relevant to the question asked or the directive given. If a response does not relate to the topic, it will score zero marks.
> Answer *all* parts of the question. Be aware that essay or short-answer questions can count in parts.
> Express yourself as clearly and logically as possible.
> Make sure your handwriting is legible.

After the exam

Reflect and learn from the exam experience

Enjoy the feelings of relief as you leave the exam venue! Congratulate yourself on having sat the examination and done the best you could do in the circumstances. You will not achieve anything by listening to others or berating yourself for not including something you may have forgotten at the time. What is done is done! Now is the time to 'let your hair down' and reward yourself. It is important to acknowledge this achievement even if you have another examination within a short period of time. Sit in the sun, have a coffee, or do something else which will bring closure before moving on, regrouping your thoughts and focusing on the next task. The time for reflection around your performance in the exam is later. *Now* is the time to socialise, go out to dinner, dance, play a game, and take some time out!

There is great value, however, in reviewing your performance; as an active learner, you will appreciate this. You have worked extremely hard to get to this point, and evaluating your performance will

enable you to build on your strengths. As an active learner, you will be interested in examining:

> how thoroughly you prepared
> which exam strategies were effective
> what strategies were less effective, and why
> how well you managed your exam nerves.

Evaluating your performance will enable you to maximise your learning in order to implement successful strategies for the future. Once you have received your examination results, you may require further feedback on the quality of your responses. Approach your lecturer to discuss your exam.

Examinations

The University requires that students enrolled in topics which are delivered on campus sit their exams on campus.

Examinations for Riverland students are held at the Riverland Campus concurrently with those held at the Sturt Precinct in Adelaide. Examination FAQs: https://students.flinders.edu.au/my-course/exams-assess-results

Chapter summary

Preparing for exams can be stressful, but by taking responsibility as an active learner and implementing effective strategies to confidently process, review, recall and apply your knowledge within exam conditions you will be better prepared, organised and less anxious. Preparation and revision for an exam is essential, and in conjunction with reflection will empower you to transition successfully to the next stage of your learning. On the one hand, the exam represents the culmination of a stage of your learning; on the other hand, it symbolises a stepping stone to the next stage. A positive attitude and an active learning approach to examinations, and indeed all your learning, will enable you to construct meaning, advance your knowledge and fulfil your long-term goals.

Summary activities

1. Explain the value of an exam.
2. What are some active learning strategies you can employ in revising for an exam?
3. What is the relevance of setting goals for your revision schedule? How might this be an advantage to you?
4. Describe a revision strategy that suits your style of learning.

Reflection

Consider your previous exam or test experiences.

» How did you feel?
» What did you learn from this situation?
» How can you apply that understanding to develop strategies to minimise exam nerves at university?

Photo credits

201 © Andresr/Shutterstock; **207** © Yuri Arcurs/Shutterstock; **211** © lightpoet/Shutterstock; **216** © ARENA Creative/Shutterstock; **220** © Stephanus Le Roux/Shutterstock; **223** © EDHAR/Shutterstock.

Answers to Exercises

Activity 2.2 (p. 77): Active voice answers

1. The nurse administered the medication.
2. The nurse used a sterile container, bandages, and scissors to dress the wound.
3. The nurse needs to check the chart, assess the patient, verify the last admininistration, and ask permission from the patient.
4. Most students who struggled to complete their degree failed the pathophysiology exam.
5. The night duty nurse caught the man with no pants on.

Activity 2.3 (p. 81): Third person voice answers

1. This is an interesting study.
2. The information is quickly forgotten.
3. Nurses should not be rude and patients need to treated with respect.
4. It is not certain that better teaching caused higher grades.
5. People may not read as many books as they used to.

Activity 3.1 (p. 129): Connecting sentences, suggested answers

Families that communicate effectively transmit messages clearly. In addition, members are free to express their feelings without fear of jeopardising their standing in the family. Thus/As a result/etc, family members can support one another and have the ability to listen, empathise, and reach out to one another in times of crisis. When the needs of family members are met/ Furthermore/etc, they are more able to reach out to meet the needs of others in society.

Conversely, messages are often communicated unclearly when patterns of communication among family members are dysfunctional. Also/ Furthermore/Moreover/etc, verbal communication may be incongruent with nonverbal messages. Power struggles may be evidenced by hostility, anger, or silence. As a result/Therefore/etc, members may be cautious in expressing their feelings because they cannot predict how others in the family will respond. When family communication is impaired/In this situation/ , the growth of individual members is stunted. Consequently/ As a consequence/ In this situation/For this reason/etc, members often turn to other systems to seek personal validation and gratification.

Activity 4.3 and 4.4 (pp. 157–59): Citing, quoting, paraphrasing, and summarising, some possible answers.

Suggested answers: CVC dressing

1. (Tollefson, 2012, p. 98)
2. "a gauze dressing covered with a transparent dressing can harbour moisture and provide an environment for bacterial growth"
3. Tollefson (2012, p. 98) describes two types of dressing – transparent and gauze – used for a central venous catheter and points out that the choice between these dressings depend on number of factors such as forming a barrier, site dryness, and micro-organism risk.
4. The main summary points you should have included are: (a) two types of CVC dressing, (b) advantages and disadvantages for each dressing type, (c) choosing the dressing to suit the patient's situation, but (d) not combining the two dressing types.

Suggested answers: Planning oral medication administration

1. (Tollefson, 2012, p. 137)
2. "contamination of the drug with traces of previous drugs"
3. Tollefson (2012, p. 137) observes that many patients will sit upright to take oral medications, some may not be able to do this and will instead need to be positioned safely on their side (but not on their back).
4. The main summary points you should have included are: (a) a number of considerations when giving oral medications, (b) how the medications will be safely given, (c) whether an assessment is needed prior to giving the drug, and (d) the appropriate delivery method of the medication.

Activity 5.1 (pp. 176-77): Creating reference list entries answer

Reference list:

Tollefson, J. (2012). *Clinical psychomotor skills: Assessment tools for nursing students* (5th ed.). South Melbourne, VIC: Cengage Learning.

In-text citation:

(Tollefson, 2012, p. 3) or

Tollefson (2012, p. 3)

Reference list:

Blackman, I., Hall, M., & Darmawan, I. G. N. (2007). Undergraduate nurse variables that predict academic achievment and clinical competence in nursing. *International Education Journal, 8*(2), 222–36.

In-text citation:

(Blackman, Hall, & Darmawan, 2007, p. 225) <u>or</u>
Blackman, Hall and Darmawan (2007, p. 225)

Reference list:

Nursing and Midwifery Board of Australia. (2008). Code of ethics for
nurses. Retrieved from http://www.nursingmidwiferyboard.gov.au/

In-text citation:

(Nursing and Midwifery Board of Australia, 2008, p. 2) <u>or</u>
Nursing and Midwifery Board of Australia (2008, p. 2)

Activity 6.1 (pp. 187-89): Locating information fast

1. resistance
2. vaccination
3. killed
4. Harris
5. immunisation
6. nation
7. measles
8. varicella
9. 12 months
10. 18 months
11. four years
12. MMR
13. 2
14. 6
15. six
16. polio
17. 21
18. 'countries' and/or 'regions'
19. outbreaks
20. 80
21. 339
22. measles
23. 500
24. 27
25. 25
26. evil spirits, witchcraft, or heat
27. 12
28. 'developmental disorders' and/or 'autism'
29. epidemiological
30. WHO
31. endemic
32. 14

References

Ambe, J. P., Omotara, B.A., & Mandu Baba, M. (2001). Perceptions, beliefs and practices of mothers in sub-urban and rural areas towards measles and measles vaccination in Northern Nigeria. *Tropical Doctor, 31*(2), 89–90.

Atherton, J. S. (2011). *Learning and teaching: Angles on learning, particularly after the schooling years.* Retrieved from http://www .learningandteaching.info/learning/bloomtax.htm.

Berman, A., Snyder, S. J., Levett-Jones, T., Dwyer, T., Hales, M., Harvey, N., . . . Stanley, D. (Eds.). (2012). *Kozier & Erb's fundamentals of nursing* (2nd Australian ed., vol. 1). Frenchs Forest, NSW: Pearson Australia.

Bishop, P. (2013). Issues in public health. In G. M. Lee & P. Bishop (Eds.), *Microbiology and infection control for health professionals* (5th ed.). Frenchs Forest, NSW: Pearson Australia.

Blackman, R. (2012). Promoting family health. In A. Berman, S. J. Snyder, T. Levett-Jones, T. Dwyer, M. Hales, N. Harvey, ... D. Stanley (Eds.), *Kozier & Erb's fundamentals of nursing.* (2nd Australian ed., vol. 1, pp. 455–468). Frenchs Forest, NSW: Pearson Australia.

Bloom, B. S. (1956). *Taxonomy of educational objectives: The classification of educational goals.* New York: David McKay.

Bradshaw, J. (2012). Historical and contemporary nursing practice. In A. Berman, S. J. Snyder, T. Levett-Jones, T. Dwyer, M. Hales, N. Harvey, . . . D. Stanley (Eds.), *Kozier & Erb's fundamentals of nursing* (2nd Australian ed., vol. 1, pp. 2–22). Frenchs Forest, NSW: Pearson Australia.

Crisp, J., & Taylor, C. (Eds.). (2013). *Potter & Perry's fundamentals of nursing* (4th ed.). Sydney: Elsevier Mosby.

College of Nursing and Health Sciences. (2013). *Evidence-based practice* [Pod]. Retrieved from http://flo.flinders.edu.au/

College of Nursing and Health Sciences. (2014). *CaseWorld*™ – Greta Balodis [Case]. Retrieved from http://flo.flinders.edu.au/

Department of Health. (2013). *National immunisation program schedule.* Retrieved from http://www.immunise.health.gov.au/internet/immunise/ publishing.nsf/Content/4CB920F0D49C61F1CA257B2600828523/$Fi le/nips-oct2013.pdf.

Elbow, P. (1998). *Writing with power: Techniques for mastering the writing process* (2nd ed.) New York: Oxford University Press.

Faigley, L. (2018). *The little Penguin handbook* (2nd ed.) Melbourne, VIC: Pearson Australia.

Gardner, H. (1993). *Multiple intelligences: The theory in practice*. New York: Basic Books.

Gillet, A. (2014). *Using English for academic purposes*. Retrieved from http://www.uefap.com/index.htm

Gillett, A., Hammond, A., & Martala, M. (2009). *Inside track to successful academic writing*. Harlow, England: Pearson Education Ltd.

Gonda, J., & Hales, M. (2012). Health care delivery systems. In A. Berman, S. J. Snyder, T. Levett-Jones, T. Dwyer, M. Hales, N. Harvey, . . . D. Stanley (Eds.), *Kozier & Erb's fundamentals of nursing* (2nd Australian ed., vol. 1, pp. 108–126). Frenchs Forest, NSW: Pearson Australia.

Grant, J. (2012). Lecture 1: Health across the lifespan. NURS 11.3 Health Promotion [Learning materials]. Retrieved from http://flo.flinders.edu.au/

Hand Hygiene Australia. (2014). *Hand hygiene*. Retrieved from http://www.hha.org.au/ForConsumers/FactSheets.aspx#Top

Hansen, E., & Beaver, S. (2012). Faculty support for ESL nursing students: Action plan for success. *Nursing Education Perspectives, 33*(4), 246–50.

Harris, P., Nagy, S., & Vardaxis, N. (2009). *Mosby's dictionary of medicine, nursing and health professions* (2nd Australian and New Zealand ed.). Chatswood, NSW: Elsevier-Mosby.

Honey, P., & Mumford, A. (1982). *The manual of learning styles*. Maidenhead, UK: Peter Honey Publications.

Kolb, V. (1984). *Experiential learning: Experience as the source of learning and development*. Englewood Cliffs, NJ: Prentice Hall.

Lave, J. L., & Wenger, E. (1998). *Communities of practice: Learning, meaning and identity*. Cambridge, UK: Cambridge University Press.

Lee, G. M., & Bishop, P. (2013). *Microbiology and infection control for health professionals* (5th ed.). Frenchs Forest, NSW: Pearson Australia.

McPherson, C., & Stakenberg, M. (2012). Values, ethics and advocacy. In A. Berman, S. J. Snyder, T. Levett-Jones, T. Dwyer, M. Hales, N. Harvey, . . . D. Stanley (Eds.), *Kozier & Erb's fundamentals of nursing* (2nd Australian ed., vol. 1, pp. 88–106). Frenchs Forest, NSW: Pearson Australia.

Müller, A. (2012). Research-based design of a medical vocabulary videogame. *International Journal of Pedagogies and Learning, 7*(2), 122–34.

Nursing and Midwifery Board of Australia. (2016). Registered nurse standards for practice. Retrieved from http://www.nursingmidwiferyboard.gov.au/

Oshima, A. & Hogue, A. (2006). *Writing academic English* (4th ed.). White Plains, NY: Pearson Longman.

Purdue University Writing Lab. (2014). *The Purdue Online Writing Lab (OWL).* Retrieved from https://owl.english.purdue.edu/owl/

Scheele, T. H., Pruit, R., Johnson, A., & Xu, Y. (2011). What do we know about educating Asian ESL nursing students? A literature review. *Nursing Education Perspectives, 32*(4), 244–249.

Scully, N. (2012). Critical thinking and the nursing process. In A. Berman, S. J. Snyder, T. Levett-Jones, T. Dwyer, M. Hales, N. Harvey, . . . D. Stanley (Eds.), *Kozier & Erb's fundamentals of nursing* (2nd Australian ed., vol. 1, pp. 192–278). Frenchs Forest, NSW: Pearson Australia.

Smith, G. C. S., & Pell, J. P. (2003). Parachute use to prevent death and major trauma related to gravitational challenge: Systematic review of randomised controlled trials. *BMJ, 327*, 1459-61. Retrieved from http://www.bmj.com/content/327/7429/1459.pdf%2Bhtml

Tollefson, J. (2012). *Clinical psychomotor skills: Assessment tools for nursing students* (5th ed.). South Melbourne, Australia: Cengage Learning.

Tuckman, B. (1965). Developmental sequence in small groups. *Psychological Bulletin, 63*(6), 384–99.

Wake, M., Harris, C., Hesketh, K., & Wright, M. (2002). *Child health screening and surveillance: A critical review of the evidence.* Retrieved from the National Health and Medical Research Council website: http://www.nhmrc.gov.au/

Index

A

abbreviations
  in academic writing style 73, 83–84
  for note taking 109
academic integrity 150
academic writing style 71–86
  overview of 86, 99
  abbreviations in 73, 83–84
  active/passive voice 73–78
  confident statements 80–81
  contractions in 71, 73, 83–84
  grammar reference texts 86
  nominalisation 78–79
  strong claims 81–83
  tentative statements 79
  third person in 71, 84–86, 94
  See also writing
active learning 27–29
  critical thinking 63–64, 180–182, 194–198
  exam revision 207–210
  importance of 2, 5–6
  independent study 44–49
  learning styles 22–26, 44–45, 183
  online 21–22
  reading See Active Reading Process
  reflection 57–63
  stress management 42–43
  study routine 36–41
  time management 33–36, 106, 203–206
  writing and 104, 107

Active Learning Approach 27–29, 36, 64, 107
active listening 52–54
Active Reading Process 185–198
  step 1: pre-reading 186
  step 2: skimming 186
  step 3: scanning 186–187
  step 4: reading for detail 193
  step 5: critical analysis 182, 194–198
active voice 73–78
adjectives
  modal 80
  overuse of 73
adverbs 73, 79, 80, 136
agreement errors 138
alternative solutions section 98
ambiguity 68
American Psychological Association style See APA referencing style
ampersands 170
analysis, critical See critical thinking
analytical approach, in case studies 97
and (connecting word) 170
APA referencing style 170–177
  in-text citations 170–171
  online guide 161
  reference lists 171–175
appendices
  in case studies 99
  in reports 96
artwork, citations for 174–175
assignments

D

dangling modifiers 138
databases 118–119
dependent clauses 68–69, 134–137
descriptive reflection 58
descriptive writing 58
Dewey, John 58
diagrams, citations for 174
dialogic reflection 58
diet 202–203
direct quotations 94, 151–153, 156, 170
disability support 8
discussion section 95
drafting 124–130

E

each (pronoun) 138
eating well 202–203
editing 131
Elbow, Peter 124
electronic resources *See* online resources
ellipsis 153
employment guidance 42
EndNote referencing software 160–161
English language development 11, 100
essays
  in exams 210–212
  references in *See* referencing
  research for 91, 107 *See also* research
  timeframe for 106
  writing guidelines 90–94

examinations
  overview of 200
  cover sheets 220–221
  handwriting skills for 207, 212
  preparation for 202–207
  process
    day before exam 218–219
    day of exam 219
    during exam 220
    reading time 220–222
    writing time 222
  purpose of 202
  reflection after 223–224
  revision for 207–210
  special consideration 217
  stress management 202–204, 218–219, 222
  support services 217
  tips for 212, 223
  types of 210–217
    essays 210–212
    multiple choice 213–214
    online tests 216–217
    open book 216
    problem-solving 214–215
    short answers 213
  university requirements 217, 224
exercise 34–35, 43
extension questions 214

F

FAN (Flinders Authentication Name) 19
financial advice 9, 42
first draft 124–130
first person 71, 84–86, 94